WALKING
WITH THE
PATRIARCHS

David Hasey

WESTBOW
PRESS®
A DIVISION OF THOMAS NELSON
& ZONDERVAN

WestBow Press books may be ordered through booksellers or by contacting:

WestBow Press
A Division of Thomas Nelson & Zondervan
1663 Liberty Drive
Bloomington, IN 47403
www.westbowpress.com
844-714-3454

ISBN: 978-1-6642-4804-5 (sc)
ISBN: 978-1-6642-4803-8 (e)

Print information available on the last page.

WestBow Press rev. date: 10/27/2021

ACKNOWLEDGEMENTS

This journey with the Patriarchs began when a good friend said one morning in the midst of a Bible study "I hate Jacob". He paused, and then said "I hate Jacob because I am Jacob". He saw himself as the scheming, self-serving manipulator that Jacob was, and didn't like it. This led to my thinking about the Patriarchs. Who really were they? What issues were they facing as they walked through ancient Canaan? How would I characterize them? How much am I just like them? In the midst of these questions I came across the blogs of Julia Blum, a Jewish Christian writer who has blogged extensively on the book of Genesis. Her insights into the characters of the Patriarchs and the inter-connectedness of the Hebrew texts have been extremely valuable as I have walked with the Patriarchs and learned from them. Many of my thoughts and reflections have germinated in her articles.

A special thanks goes to Ellen Davis whose editorial
skills corrected issues of grammar and style.

INTRODUCTION

Imagine that you are a married woman, aged 65. You have just celebrated your golden anniversary. Although your husband and you had hoped for a large family, you were unable to have children. Although you are religious, you don't have a relationship with the God of the Bible. One afternoon your 75-year-old husband comes home and says the following. "Honey, we are selling the house, buying a tent to live in, forfeiting the family land and inheritance, and taking off for … actually, I don't know where we are going. A God told me that if I do this he will bless me and give me children and I will be a blessing to others!" How would you respond? Would you say, "Let's go" and start packing? Or would you call 911? Would you believe him or wonder about his sanity? This is effectively what Sarah faced when God called Abraham to step out in faith. We don't know how she responded, as the biblical text is silent about that. We only know that she went with him, whether from receiving a call as well, out of dependency on Abraham for survival, out of guilt at being barren, or something else. But as they moved at least nine times over the course of several years she had to wonder. The hope and belief that all of the promised descendants would come through her had to loom large. But it would be one which seemed less and less hopeful as time passed and there was no child.

In the book of Genesis there are three major characters: Adam, Noah, and Abraham. After the fall into sin and the resulting depravity of mankind, God begins again with Noah. After the debacle at the Tower of Babel, he begins again with Abraham.

Our story begins on the global scene, then narrows down to the Middle East, until it focuses on the city of Ur of the Chaldeans. It narrows further to one particular family, the family of Terah and his three sons, who according to Joshua worshipped multiple gods at the time (Jos 24:2, 14). Finally it hones in on Terah's eldest son, Abram, or as we more popularly know him, Abraham. But it doesn't end there. It expands again, first to his small nuclear family and the families of his son and grandson. A large family immigrates to Egypt where its descendants live for several centuries. Upon leaving Egypt, it widens to incorporate a nation—Israel, before again encompassing the entire world, as seen in the blessing of Abram. Who are these people—Abram and his wife Sarai, Isaac and his wife Rebekah, Jacob and his wives Leah and Rachel and their children? What can we learn by looking at their lives, lived some 2,500 – 3,000 years ago? The majority of the book of Genesis provides clues and answers to these questions.

We begin with Genesis chapter 11:27: "Now these are the records of the generations of Terah." The Hebrew word *toledoth,* often translated "generations," occurs several times in Genesis. In Gen 5:1 it introduces the descendants of Adam, culminating in Noah, with the phrase "the *toledoth*" of Adam. In Gen 11:10 the descendants of Shem are introduced, culminating in Terah. In Gen 11:27 it introduces the descendants of Terah, specifically Abram. Other than serving as an introduction to Abram, is there any significance to the section beginning with Terah instead of Abram? I think so.

The same Hebrew phrase "They set out to go to the land of Canaan" occurs in both Gen 11:31 and Gen 12:5. In the first case it refers to Terah and his family, in the second to Abram and his family. Both initially set out for Canaan, but only Abram follows through. When we couple the same Hebrew phraseology in both Terah's and Abram's decision to go to Canaan, with the unlikely nature of Terah's up and leaving Ur on his own, it appears something deeper is going on. Although the Bible doesn't say so, there is the suggestion that perhaps God's call first came to Terah.[1] Laban hints at Yahweh, the God of Abraham, as being Terah's God as well (Gen 31:53). Terah responded by getting up and starting for Canaan. But he stopped in Haran. Life in the city may have seemed better than wandering around the land of Canaan in a tent. And so he missed out on the blessing that God intended to give him. The call to Abram is recorded because he totally responded to God's call!

Reflection and Application —————————————————————————————————

There is a lesson for us when we place Terah and Abram side by side. We all long to have an encounter with God as Abram and perhaps Terah did. But having such an encounter is not what defines us. Don't forget Adam and Eve had an encounter with God as well, which ended in disobedience. What defines us is what we do in response to the encounters we receive. Unless we respond in faithfulness and obedience we will become like Terah, never becoming what we could and should become. What a pity!

This is what faith is about: starting and then completing whatever we are called to do, even if it causes adversity. It points to a spiritual law we should never forget. "We choose our destiny by the way we respond to God's call."[2] Although in Abram's case it was a pretty big call, our call might be something more minor. It may be some little thing that God uses to test our faithfulness for greatness in his kingdom. It could even be something as mundane as faithfully taking out the garbage. Will we be faithful to what we hear from God for our lives?

Why are the stories of the Patriarchs included in the Bible? To answer this question we must look at who would have first heard these stories – the Children of Israel who were wandering through the wilderness. After their exodus from Egypt and the long forty-year journey through the wilderness they couldn't help wondering "Who are we"? What is our purpose? The stories of the Patriarchs helped give them that answer. They could answer, "Just like the Patriarchs, we are God's chosen people." Though they often failed, they were still chosen and blessed by him. Though we often fail, he has still chosen and blesses us as well." God has chosen us, members of his Church, as his people. Like them we have often failed. Yet he still loves us. As he called the Patriarchs and redeemed their descendants, so he also has called and redeemed us.

As we read the Scriptures we discover God's interaction with his world and the people in it. We see them sometimes exhibiting faithfulness, other times not. The Bible presents both. We tend to think of the Patriarchs as great men of faith. A closer look at them and their wives presents a different picture than we usually imagine. The patriarchs were far from perfect. They were much like we are. They could lie with the best of them. They were manipulators and thieves. They struggled with jealousy and impatience. All failed as parents, showing favoritism to their children. Jacob was a schemer par excellence. At times their eyes were blind to what God was doing. In showing us their lives the Bible presents the good, the bad, and the ugly. There are many things about them that we would not want to emulate. But throughout their long lives they were always open to God, allowing him to lead them. They didn't have a static faith; it continued to grow stronger as they struggled with the experiences of life and God's dealing with them. As we look at their lives we will see their growing faith. This is something we can and should emulate. Throughout our walk with the Patriarchs there are several Reflection and Application thoughts and questions. Keeping a journal of your thoughts and answers to the questions might aid you in your own walk. Use these reflections in your prayer time.

Reflection and Application

Is my faith settled or is it still growing? Am I open to God as the Patriarchs and their wives were? As we look at their lives, compare yourself with them. How do I see myself doing the things they did?

CHAPTER 1

Abraham and Sarah

GOD'S CALL TO ABRAM (GEN 12:1-9)

The name "Abram" is a compound of two Hebrew words *ab* (father) and *ram* (exalted), meaning "exalted father." The irony of his name is that he is not a father! Each time he heard his name called, it would have reminded him of his lack of a son.

The genealogies in the earlier part of Genesis contain a series of "begats." They go on and on; so and so became the father of who became the father of. But when we come to Abram and Sarai there is a sudden stop. The Hebrew text makes a significant point to announce that Sarai is barren (Gen 11:30). The same will be true of Rebekah and Rachel as well. For a woman to be barren in that culture was a sign of the displeasure of the gods. It was the cause of great despair, even guilt. The desperateness of the barren condition is poignantly shown in the prayer of Hannah for a child (I Sam 1). Why is Sarai's barrenness important to the story? It points to the miraculous birth of her son which we will come to in time.

Given that in that culture people married young, it is likely that Abram and Sarai had already been married for fifty-plus years when Abram heard God's call. Abram had been hoping and pining for a son year after year, decade after decade. With his infertile wife approaching or having reached the end of her childbearing years, God's call to him could have seemed like a cruel joke. To leave a settled life for a nomadic one late in one's life on the basis of an impossible promise doesn't make a lot of sense. Yet Abram believed God, pulled up stakes, and with his wife, nephew, and all his retainers took off for an unknown destination. This is the basis of faith: To take action on account of belief.

It is likely that Abram did not yet have the intimate connection with God that we see in the coming chapters of Genesis. Yet he is willing to break all of his previous religious ties. In the cultural times of his day the great gods had little personal contact with individuals. Individuals would more likely worship local deities as family gods. By leaving Haran for Canaan, Abram abandons all of the geographical, political and ethnic related gods. By adhering to Yahweh's call, Abram stakes his future on God alone. [3]

We don't know exactly why God chose Abram, as scripture is silent regarding this. There are two interpretations often suggested. The Christian interpretation suggests that it had nothing to do with Abram's merits. He was merely a recipient of God's grace. The Jewish interpretation has a different slant. They consider Abram to be like Noah, a righteous man. For this reason God chose him out.

Reflection and Application ———

Despite having the Scriptures and the Holy Spirit, there is much about God that we don't know. Are we as willing as Abram to stake our claim on him, to honor him and worship him?

Are there times in my life where God has called me to step out in faith? Is God calling me to step out in faith at the moment? Am I willing to change course, to step out when it doesn't appear to make any sense? Am I willing to risk everything for God? We will touch on this more in the sections below.

Genesis 12:1-3 are known as the Abrahamic covenant, although the word covenant doesn't occur until Genesis 15:18. We will talk more about the covenant at that point.

THE NATURE OF GOD'S CALL

There is much in God's call to Abram that doesn't make rational sense. Abram was elderly, though given that he lived to age 125 it's possible he might have still been in the prime of life at age 75. He would have to leave a comfortable life in Haran to go to an unknown place. There were three societal comforts he had to give up–his country, his family and his father's house. He couldn't even leave a forwarding address! If he does what God asks of him, God promises to do three things. He will make of Abram a great nation, he will bless him with favor and make his name great, and Abram will be a blessing to others, even to all the families of the earth. But Sarai is unable to have children, so how is that going to work out? Abram, in faith, responds to God's call, to a God who since he likely had been a polytheist, he didn't know very well, and sets out. It is only because he does so that he receives the blessing.

One of the most famous phrases in the Old Testament occurs in Gen 12:1. *Lech Lecha* is a phrase that means literally "Go to you" or "Go to yourself." "Going" in the Hebrew Bible has the sense of "going towards ones ultimate purpose or service to God." This is what Abram is called to: to find that purpose for which he was created. He was to leave his heathen background and go. In his going he would have a continued growth towards holiness. Along the way there would be reversals and setbacks, yet that progression towards holiness would continue. In the process he was to spread God's name. This is how he would be a blessing.

He was called to leave three things: his country, his relatives, and his father's house. The order in which he is called to leave goes from the easiest to the hardest. It might not have been emotionally difficult to leave his country, but it would have been very difficult to leave his father's house. As Terah's heir, that meant giving up the land acquired by his father and his property that he inherited. He was giving up everything that would have meant security.

Reflection and Application —————————————————————————————

Thus their adventure of walking with God began. It is an adventure that God desires all of us to begin and continue through life. We are all called by God. It may be early in life as in the case of Jeremiah who was called before he was born (Jer 1:5) or it may be late in life as was true of Abraham. We are all called to a continued movement towards holiness. Like Abraham we are called to be a blessing to others. This can be done by sharing the gospel. It can also be done by not causing the gospel to be shamed (Ps 69:6). It can be done through serving the poor. Have I ever sensed God calling me in any particular way? If not, ask him to show you. If you have, share this with others. Abraham was willing to risk everything for God. The disciples left everything behind to follow Jesus. What am I willing to risk or give up to embrace the claim of God on my life?

The Hebrew verb "to bless" also has the meaning of "to kneel." It is also related to the nouns "blessing" and "knee." One who bends the knee in service becomes a blessing to others. At the same time he is blessed by serving.

Reflection and Application ————————————————————————————

We are called to serve others. Jesus tells his disciples that the one who will be considered great among them is the one who will serve them, and reminds them that he came to serve, not to be served (Mt 20:25-28). St Paul tells us to humbly serve one another in love (Gal 5:13). Are there times when I have felt blessed when serving someone? What about the event led to my feeling blessed?

THE BLESSING OF ABRAM (GEN 12:2-3)

There are three aspects of the blessing of Abram that are important. First, as seen in Deuteronomy 28, the continuation of the blessing given to Abram is dependent upon their faithfulness to God. Second, Abram and his descendants will be a blessing to others because they are favored by God. Third, through Abram and his descendants God will bless all the people of the earth. This third aspect is unconditional, and has come to fruition through the work of Jesus upon the cross.

THE PLACE OF WORSHIP (GEN 12:7-8)

When Abram finally reaches Canaan he stops at the oak of Moreh. God speaks to him again (Gen 12:7). Abram's response is to build an altar to worship at. The Hebrew text hints that this is where Abram may have begun to truly worship God. The last part of verse 7 in

Hebrew reads slightly different than the English translations do: "And he built an altar to Yahweh, the one who had appeared to him." The phrase "who had appeared" is a participle with the definite article, singling out which particular God. As he settles in the area between Bethel and Ai he again builds an altar and worships by calling on the name of the Lord. These examples show us the proper response to hearing from God–worship!

In this account we again see a veiled connection with Adam and Noah. Adam failed to care for the land he was given and was cast out on the east side of the Garden of Eden (Gen 3:24). Abram is also given land to care for, settling east of Bethel (Gen 12:8). The name Bethel means "house of God". Eden was the sanctuary of God. Like Noah Abram builds an altar to worship the Lord (Gen 8:20-21). The relationship that God establishes with Abram will continue throughout the Bible through the covenant.

Reflection and Application ————————————————————————————

We have the great opportunity to hear God through his word and Spirit. We hear his word in the lectionary readings of the day each time we attend church. At times we feel led by his Spirit to a particular action. We are fed through the Eucharist. Our heartfelt response should be praise and worship. But we can find ourselves seeing this as something routine. We hear the Scriptures read in church. We receive the Eucharist. Do we naturally turn to praise and worship or do look at our watches wondering how soon the service will be over?

THE CHANGE OF NAMES

It will take another 24 years before Abram's and Sarai's names will be changed. Why does God wait all these years to enact their name changes? They weren't ready to receive new names. God had to first perform a work in their lives. They needed healing before they were ready. Sarah would have to become dependent on God first. Abraham had to truly believe that God would really give him a son by Sarah, and later be willing to sacrifice his so longed-for only beloved son. But first, God had to bring healing to their lives.

THE DESCENT TO EGYPT (GEN 12:10-20)

Not long after they reached Canaan there was a severe famine. This would have been devastating for Abram, having large herds. You can almost hear Sarai asking, "Tell me again why we left Haran for this dreary place?" As a result of the famine they descend to an area of Egypt that had not experienced the famine, coming under the notice of Pharaoh. In the account (Gen 12:10-20) we see a side of Abram that is totally incongruent with his being a man of faith. He is afraid for his life! Despite the experience of receiving his wonderful call from God, despite the fact that he left Haran at God's call and promise in total faith, despite his belief that God will give him children, he doesn't believe God will protect him! He takes matters into his own hands. What happened to the great faith he exhibited a short while before? He is willing to abandon Sarai in order to attempt to save his life. He lies about his relationship with her. In the culture of the day, it was considered a great sacrilege to take another man's wife into one's harem or as a wife, but not so if the husband was dead. Abram's fear is that Pharaoh will have him killed, making it OK for him to acquire Sarai, much as David did to Uriah the Hittite when he took Bathsheba as a wife.

In his weakness, Abram thought only of himself, not thinking of what effect his suggestion would have on Sarai and their relationship with each other. For his own safety he was willing to allow her to be violated by Pharaoh. He began to think through Egyptian eyes. We don't know Sarai's thoughts on the matter, for the Bible is silent on that. But it appears she reluctantly went along with Abram's scheme, for in Gen 12:15 Sarai is taken into Pharaoh's harem. We do know, however, that she did say something. As a result God sent plagues upon Pharaoh and his house. The translations say this was "because of Sarai, Abram's wife" (Gen 12:17 NASB, NAB, NIV). The Hebrew text says something different: "because of the word of Sarai, Abram's wife." Her word, whatever she said, prophetically anticipates another descent into Egypt and ascent out of it. It also anticipates another set of plagues sent by God, through Moses, upon another Pharaoh (Ex 7:14 – 12:32).

This may be the point where God begins to bring spiritual healing to Sarai. Not only is Yahweh the God who has called and blessed her husband, he is also her comforter and protector, someone she can count on as well. The lesson has begun, but will not sink in for many more years.

Abram's descent into Egypt can be considered a spiritual descent as he exhibits a lack of faith and falls into sin. It is a sort of exile. While the text doesn't say that God told him not to go down to Egypt, it clearly says he went "down" to Egypt. It is a reversal of the spiritual journey he is on. In going down to Egypt Abram abandons the land which God has given him. He will have to ascend up out of Egypt to continue his spiritual journey.

Whether his going to Egypt was disobedience of not, God uses this time to draw Abram closer to him. He is in a better place with God afterwards as we will see in Genesis 15.

Reflection and Application

Temptations often come after great moments of faith. Satan doesn't want us to succeed. He wants us to fail so he can accuse us. Despite his failure in Egypt, Abram is still known as a man of faith. Despite David's many failures he was still known as a man after God's own heart. It is good to remember that we may be most vulnerable to Satan's attack right after having a mountaintop experience with God. It is a time we should especially pray and seek the prayer support of others. Despite our failures, we can also be men and women of faith. The key is to confess and repent when we fail, receiving absolution from our sins. We should always be seeking to have an intimate relationship with Jesus, unlike Adam and Eve who turned away from God.

When we take matters into our own hands, as Abram did, we often go against the plan of God, with negative results. The only proper response when we do so is to confess the sin and seek absolution.

Just as Abram was, we are also on a spiritual journey. Like him, we will often take one step back for every two forward. The God, who was with Abram all through his journey is the same one who is with us, guiding and leading us. How many times do I see through secular eyes instead of eyes of faith? Pray to be open to God's leading.

We are living in exile from God due to our sin. Sin requires redemption if we are to become reconnected to God. The acknowledgement of our sin and the recognition of the supreme sacrifice of Christ on the cross for us leads us to a greater love for him than we might otherwise have.

ABRAM AND LOT (GEN 13)

Digging into the text tells us numerous things about both Abram and Lot. We know that Lot's father had died back in Ur (Gen 11:28). We don't know whether or not Lot's mother was still alive. That the names of both of his aunts are mentioned while his mother's name is not suggests he may have been an orphan. Abram's taking his nephew Lot with him suggests he may have treated him similarly to a son. In this we see the compassionate side of Abram, something we will see over and over again. We know that both Abram and Lot were wealthy, possessing large herds of livestock and herdsmen, so many that when together the land couldn't support both (Gen 13:6-7). It points to God's faithfulness in blessing Abram as well as blessing others (Lot). In Abram's decision to separate from Lot we again see his compassion and generosity. He refuses to claim the best land for himself, allowing Lot to choose (Gen 13:8-12). He is also shown to be a peaceful man. His decision to separate is based on the desire for peace (Gen 13:8-9). He had every right to claim all the land for himself, for God had promised it to him, and reiterates this promise just a few verses later when he tells Abram that all the land that he can see to the north, south, east, and west will be his (Gen 13:14-18). Yet Abram is willing to forego this claim for the sake of peace.

Reflection and Application ————————————————————————————————

Are we men and women of compassion, generosity and peace? Are we more like Abraham or Lot? What would be my tendency if I found myself in Abram's place? Would I have done the same as he did? Do I have the same conviction of things not seen?

Lot, on the other hand, appears to be greedy. Given the option, he takes the best for himself. It was a lush land, a reflection of the Garden of Eden (Gen 13:10-11). By his action he demonstrates a lack of generosity. He isn't described as being evil. Lot chooses based on what he can see (Gen 13:10) while Abram demonstrates his faith as described in Hebrews based on the conviction and hope of what was not seen (Heb 11:1, 8-9). Lot's decision comes from the pride of the eyes. The land he saw looked good. While looking good, as we will see in the coming chapters of Genesis, it actually wasn't. Sodom was a cesspool of sin.

How often do we find ourselves doing things similar to what Lot did—looking at the surface instead of what is inside? Are there decisions I have made that I initially thought were good, but later proved not to be? How did they turn out? What spiritual lesion can I learn from the experiences?

On another level, the division between Abram and Lot was necessary. As long as both were in the land, Lot and his descendants could lay claim to it. After the division from Lot God entreats Abram to look around him. The four directions of the compass have geographical orientations. North points to Mt Tsaphon on the border between modern Syria and Turkey. South points to the Negev desert area. West points to the Mediterranean Sea (the Hebrew word effectively means "seaward"). East points to going back towards something earlier—in this case Eden. Unlike the modern world where we orient everything towards north, in the biblical world the orientation was east. God tells Abram that all he can see will be given to him and his descendants (Gen 13:14-18)

The text notes that the men of Sodom where Lot settled were exceedingly wicked (Gen 13:12-13). Not the best place to live. Is there evidence that Lot himself was corrupted by the Sodomites? Not directly. As we will see later, he takes a strong stand against their wickedness (Gen 19:1-10). After his separation from Abram he moved in the direction of Sodom (Gen 13:2). But by Genesis 19 he is living in Sodom. That the angels found him sitting at the gate suggests he had become one of Sodom's leaders (Gen 19:1). The men of Sodom request Lot to produce the men whom he has housed so that they can know them. The Hebrew word *yada`* (know) often has sexual connotations. It is the word used in Gen 4:1 for the birth of Cain. Lot's strong objection to their request highly suggests that the men of Sodom had such thoughts in their mind. In an attempt to appease them Lot is willing to allow them to rape his daughters (Gen 19:8). Peter calls Lot righteous because of his stance against them. He has his own moral issues in suggesting that the men rape his daughters instead. He flees Sodom with only the clothes on his back (Gen 19:15-17). His wife and two sons–in–law die in the conflagration (Gen 19:14, 26). In the end we see him hiding out in a cave with his daughters, both of whom conceive a child by him (Gen 19:19-38). He was spared from the destruction that overtook Sodom by the mercy that God granted to Abraham.

Lot's example points to the difficulty in living a moral life when we see sin happening all around us. His wife and sons-in-laws succumb in the destruction. He was unable to have a righteous impact on them. His daughters commit immoral acts themselves. By totally separating himself from Abram he cut himself off from the family of God. There is great value in being connected to the Church and other Christians in such times.

ABRAM AND MELCHIZEDEK (GEN 14)

The story of Abram and Melchizedek is one of the most enigmatic stories in the Bible. Melchizedek is mentioned only four times in the Bible; here in Genesis, in Psalms 110:4, in Hebrews 5:6, 10, and in Hebrews 7. Only Genesis tells us anything about him. He was both the king of Salem and a priest of the God Most High. The story begins with Lot and his family being captured in a war against the kings of Sodom and Gomorrah. In Abram's response we again see his compassionate nature. We also see him as a man who doesn't hold a grudge. He could have said to himself, "It serves Lot right for taking the best land for himself." But upon learning of Lot's capture, he acts as his brother's keeper, unlike Cain with Abel (Gen 4:9). Abram and his men embark on a 200 mile journey to rescue Lot. He was willing to take the time, the expense, and the risk to free Lot. We also see that he had friendly relations with those living around him, for they join him (Gen 14:13, 24). Upon his return he meets two people, Bera, the king of Sodom and Melchizedek. These two individuals couldn't be more different. The name of the king of Sodom means "in evil." The name of his companion king Birsha, king of Gomorrah, means "in wickedness". In contrast, Melchizedek means "My king is righteous."

The Hebrew text says in Gen 14:20 "and he gave him a tenth of all". It is unclear who either the giver or the receiver is. The traditional view is that Abram gave a tenth of the plunder he obtained to Melchizedek. There are two aspects of this encounter that are equally important. Of first importance is the fact that God, not Abram, is described as obtaining the victory. Second is Abram's refusal to profit from the victory. He had every right, in the custom of the day, to have taken the entire spoils for himself. Bera tempts him with this, telling him to keep the plunder. As a person of integrity, he refuses to take advantage of the situation for his personal gain. He only asks that those who went with him can take their share.

Abram refuses to take even something as worthless as a used shoestring (Gen 14:22-23). He desires that God alone receive the honor for making him prosperous. His action is one of great humility. John the Baptist, in humility, says something very similar when comparing himself with Christ (Jn 1:27). Though a prophet, he notes that he is unworthy of doing something even as menial as tying Jesus' shoe. In Abram's actions we see the two greatest commandments enacted: love of God and love of neighbor.

Abram has a choice presented to him. Melchizedek and Bera meet him at the Valley of Shaveh (Gen 14:17). Shaveh, in Hebrew, has the meaning of "equal" or "worth." In modern Hebrew the saying "to reach the Valley of Shaveh" means to reach a compromise.[4] Abram is given a test in this valley. Will he compromise his integrity and his faith? Will he accept righteousness or evil? Abram passes the test, choosing righteousness. In the Valley of Shaveh he makes a worthy choice. He chooes to give to Melchizedek instead of taking everything for himself.

Reflection and Application ——————————————————————————————————————

There are times when we, like Abram, will be tested. Many times the options before us can seem to be almost equal. But one may have its root in evil while the other has its root in righteousness. We will then face the challenge of deciding which to accept. These are the times when our principles, our integrity, and our faith must enter the picture. How we view these traits may be the deciding factor. They will help us see which choice is worthy. This is why it is important to decide what principles we will not compromise, how important our integrity is, and how essential our faith in God is.

There is another lesson to be learned if Melchizedek is the giver by comparing Abram's response to the two kings. One is a king of righteousness, the other a king of evil. Abram is willing to receive from the king of righteousness but will not countenance evil.

In the Dead Sea Scroll 11QMelch Melchizedek is presented as an eschatological savior, begotten in his mother's womb by the Word of God. The book of Hebrews picks up on this theme in the New Testament (Heb 7).

There are times when we have the opportunity to do something which is lawful for us to do, but is not for the best. It may harm someone else. It is in times like these that we can put into demonstrative practice the love of neighbor. How will others be affected by my actions? It can be very tempting when the action might benefit us. But to carry it out indicates a lack of trust in God, effectively saying that he is not capable of caring for us. In Abram and John the Baptist we see great humility, leading them to avoid anything that might advance themselves either materially or in status. Are we as ready to be that humble as we go through life? Are we willing to wait on God?

Generosity, humility, and love are closely related. It is love which enables a person to be generous. We see this in Abram's love and care for Lot. A generous person is always a humble person, not seeking recognition for his or her generosity. Jesus speaks to this in the Sermon on the Mount when he cautions us to give in secret. True generosity cares nothing for oneself. How well do I pass the love and humility test?

What is my relationship with things connected with evil? Am I willing to profit from such activity even if I'm not directly connected with it? This is the test Abram successfully passed. Have I done so as well?

We learn several things about Abram's character in chapter 14. First, he shows loyalty. He goes to the aid of Lot through personal risk to his life to do battle with those who had taken Lot. Second, he goes out of his way, travelling about 160 miles to rescue Lot. Third, he refuses to profit from the misfortune that occurred to Lot. He refused to take advantage of a crisis.

Reflection and Application ————————————————

It has been often noted that governments often use crises to increase their power. As Christians, we should never take advantage of difficult situations for personal gain. Right now we are experiencing the Covid-19 pandemic. How am I responding to it? Am I looking for things that I can use to benefit myself, or am I seeking ways that I can serve others in its midst?

ESTABLISHING THE COVENANT (GEN 15)

In Genesis 15 we see the progression of Abram's faith. For the first time he speaks to God. We begin to see intimacy between Abram and God developing. God has just told him that his reward will be great. Abram twice reminds God that he has no children, making sure God hears his complaint. He reminds God that a servant will be his heir. The Hebrew text emphasizes Abram's bitterness, resentment, pain, and frustration. The Hebrew words for "curse" and "childless" are homonyms that sound alike (*ariri*) but are spelled differently. Spelled with the letter *ayin* it means "childless, abandoned, and the like. Spelled with the letter *aleph* it means cursed. You can almost hear the pain in Abram's voice saying "I am cursed by being childless and you are talking about reward?!"[5] God in comforting him states clearly that Abram's own son will be his heir, asking him to count the stars, the vastness of which will be his descendants.

Although he is now 85 years old he believes God, as stated in the well known verse "Then he believed in the LORD; and He reckoned it to him as righteousness." (Gen 15:6). He still didn't understand what God's plan was in all of this as the events of chapter 16 clearly indicate. He greatly desired a child, and God said he would have one. He latched on to that promise in faith.

Verse 5 contains the Hebrew word *na'* which is sometimes translated "now". It is connected to the imperative verb "look up", emphasizing the importance of taking the action of looking up. The two words together have the sense of entreaty. Abram's compassionate God says "Look up, please". Because Abram did so, trusting in the word of God, it was accounted to him as righteousness. In Hebrew "faith" and "belief" are always tied to action and behavior. Belief is more than a mental assent. It is an act of faith and reliance on God's character.

What is the nature of Abram's faith? Does he believe God or believe in God? The King James and the New American Standard versions translate verse 6 "he believed in the Lord". The New International and Revised Standard versions translate it "he believed the Lord." The difference in translations comes from how to translate the occurrence of the name of God with the preposition often translated "in". There are times however, especially when the combination is used in reference to belief that the preposition indicates the direct object (in this case, God). Belief in God implies a belief system. Believing God implies complete trust. That is the nature of Abram's faith at this point. He categorically trusts that what God has told him is true. God considers his belief as righteousness. As a result he formally establishes his covenant with Abram.[6]

Reflection and Application ⸺

Believing God is far different than believing in God. I can believe in God without trusting him. Embracing faith involves taking God at his word, trusting him. In many ways we are all like the father of the demon possessed boy who cries out to Jesus "I believe, help my unbelief! (Mk 9:24) How would I characterize my faith? Do I believe him as well as believe in him? Am I willing to stake my life on him?

It is easy to wish we had the direct communication with God which Abram had. But in the one hundred years between God's first call to Abram and his death God only speaks directly to Abraham eight times, averaging once every twelve and a half years. There were long periods of silence. Years pass until God speaks again. In a way these were Abram's dark nights of the soul – wondering when God's promise to him would come about. It was his trust in God that carried him through these dark periods.

Reflection and Application ⸺

Like Abram we all at some point in our lives experience that dark night of the soul. God seems very far away and unreachable. Our prayers to him feel as though they are bouncing off the ceiling back at us. These are the times when trusting God carries us through. It is helpful at such times to remember our history with God, to reflect on what all he has done for us. When have I felt the dark night of the soul in my life? What has helped me through those times?

In the eyes of modern civilization the covenant enactment in Genesis 15 seems very strange. What is going on? To a person living back then the description would have been very common and extremely meaningful. For Abram it would have totally confirmed God's promise and his character. Several different kinds of covenants were known. They all had the same format. Most covenants were bilateral, between two kings or between a king and a vassal. Some were unilateral. Each party of the covenant would agree to certain stipulations binding them to fulfill. The greater king would protect his vassal and the vassal promised obedience. The slain animals were an object lesson. The animals were drawn and quartered, the two halves separated. The two people enacting the covenant would walk between them, meeting in the middle. The covenantal oath contained wording to the effect that if either party violated the covenant may he become like this torn apart animal.

The covenant in Genesis 15 is unilateral. Abram is asleep. Only God, as a flaming torch passes through, promising the land to Abram's descendants. We are still left with the question of what exactly the covenant expresses. To understand this we must look at the nature of the polytheistic religions of the ancient world. Their gods were connected to the forces of nature. For example, within the Ugaritic pantheon there were gods of fertility, the sea (representing chaos) and death. The Philistine god Dagon was a god of grain (crop fertility). These gods all had one feature in common: they didn't reveal their natures so that their worshippers knew what would bring them the god's favor or wrath. "They were worshipped by being flattered, cajoled, humored, and appeased."[7] Their worshippers were constantly trying to manipulate them in order to be treated well. I remember once reading an old Babylonian text where a worshipper was complaining about how his god was treating him. He said, in effect "If you don't start treating me better I'll stop bringing you food, and then where will you be!"

God, in establishing the covenant, declares himself to be a personal God, a God of relationships. He enters into a relationship with Abram who responds with faith and trust. He doesn't require that Abram first give up the polytheistic beliefs he brought with him. But he does offer to give Abram something provided Abram will follow him. It will take more time for Abram's trust in God to grow more fully.

Reflection and Application ───────────────────────────────────

Three persons in the Bible ask the question "How can this be?" – Abram, Zacharias, and Mary. In Zacharias' case his question is one of doubt. In Mary's and Abram's case it is a question of believing faith, seeking clarification while fully trusting in God. It is OK for us to question God as long as our questions are based on believing trust in God.

Some people believe that if they are doing God's will he will automatically bless them. This view is often called the prosperity gospel. That is certainly not true in Abram's life. He had to wait for 25 years before Sarai had a son. He had to leave his home because of a severe famine. He will have to abandon his elder son. If he believed in the prosperity gospel he had every reason to abandon his faith and return to the polytheistic worship of his ancestors. Others may have a belief that to be in God's will they must suffer. Neither are true, although both may occur. God may materially bless us, or he may not. He may allow us to suffer for the purpose of drawing closer to him, or he may not. There is no discernible pattern as each person is different in their needs, desires, temptations and spiritual health. When God says his ways are not our ways it doesn't mean that his way oppose ours, it merely means they are different. We don't have the mind of God.

God calls us into a relationship with himself just as he did Abram. He established a New Covenant with us through the work of Christ on the cross. Just as he did with Abram, he accepts us just as we are and aids us in growing closer to him. How have I seen this process working in my own life?

While Abram was asleep God spoke to him about the future, telling him he would never personally inherit the land God had promised to him. It would take another four hundred years before his descendants would possess it. In the meantime they would be enslaved in a foreign nation for these four hundred years. Although the country is not mentioned, we know from the book of Exodus that they were enslaved in Egypt. God told him that they would return to claim the land in the fourth generation. The reason why this would happen is the most interesting: "The iniquity of the Amorite is not yet complete" (Gen 15:16).[8] In a way this speaks to the loving nature of God. He gives the inhabitants of Canaan 400 years to repent of their evil ways before finally punishing them through the conquest by Joshua.

Reflection and Application ———————————————————————————————————

How often do we have expectations of God that are not realized, at least not in the time frame we expect them? He's told he won't personally inherit the Promised Land. As we will see in the next chapter his expectation of having a son has gone awry. It is in times like these that we discover much about the character of our faith. Does my disappointment when things don't go as expected draw me closer to God or turn me farther away? Relationships live in the present while expectations dwell in the future. Do I pay attention to current relationships or am I driven by future expectations?

God is not willing that any should perish (II Pet 3:9). Yet he will not let evil go unpunished. He is consistent in blessing good and punishing evil (Jer 18:7-10).

The biblical use of covenant describes the relationship between God and Abram, and later with Israel, has a different focus that the secular covenants did. It does have the promise of God's protection and the requirement of Israel's obedience. It establishes a relationship between God and man. Through the stipulations of the covenant humanity begins to see what God is like.

Reflection and Application ⎯⎯⎯⎯⎯⎯⎯⎯⎯⎯⎯⎯⎯⎯⎯⎯⎯⎯⎯⎯⎯⎯⎯⎯⎯⎯

One of the greatest reasons for studying the Bible is our ability to discover more of what God is like. His character and nature are found throughout both the Old and New Testaments. What do I look for when I read Scripture? Am I looking to see more of God or something else?

SARAI AND HAGAR (GEN 16)

The Bible doesn't tell us of the enormous pain that Sarai experienced in her inability to have children. But it must have been intense. Besides the personal desire to have children, their lack was seen as a punishment from God. The lack of progeny was a major concern in the ancient world. It's certainly behind her decision to give Hagar, her handmaid to Abram in order to have a child. After fifty years of marriage without children, then another ten years after Abram's call having gone by without the promised child, she is desperate. You can hear the desperateness in her words to Abram "Perhaps I shall obtain children through her." (Gen 16:2). Sarai takes matters into her own hands to come up with a solution. She knows that Abraham was chosen by God to be the father of a nation. But it's not happening. The covenant promise of children appears to be in jeopardy. So she decides to help God.[9] In the account, the writer of Genesis links the decision of Sarai with the decision of Eve in the Garden of Eden. The same Hebrew words appear in both stories. Eve **took** of the fruit and **gave** unto her husband. Sarai **took** Hagar her maid the Egyptian and **gave** her to her husband. Just as the forbidden fruit of the tree was Eve's desire, so also Hagar became the forbidden fruit of Sarai's desire to have children. As Eve took the fruit and gave it to Adam, Sarai took Hagar and gave her to Abram. Both Eve and Sarai in their desire did something outside of God's will. For Sarai and Abram, Hagar and Ishmael, it led to further pain. The Hebrew of Gen 16:2 says "Perhaps I shall be built from her." Sarai uses the same word that is used in the story of the Tower of Babel – "Let us build". Both have disastrous results.

We see this in Genesis 16. Notice what happens once it becomes known that Hagar has conceived. Hagar views her pregnancy as a sign of being blessed by a god while Sarai has not. The closeness that Sarai and Hagar had had is gone. They experience a change in status. That Hagar is the mother to be, not Sarai adds to her grief. She then treats Hagar so harshly that she flees from Sarai, heading back to Egypt, only returning at the intervention of an angel.

Hagar views this encounter with the angel as an encounter with God himself. Most translations of Genesis 16:13, while maintaining the sense of the verse, ignore the significance of the Hebrew word translated "back". Literally, Hagar says "Here have I seen the back of him who sees me." This recalls the account of Moses seeking to see God (Ex 33:18-23) where God says he can only see his back. In Hagar's time of need, God made himself known to her.

Reflection and Application ———————————————————————————————
As in the case of God meeting Hagar in her time of need, God meets with us in our times of need as well. But we often only see his back as well. It is afterwards that we realize he has been there helping us.

Three things occur in the story of Sarah and Hagar. The covenant promise is in jeopardy because there is no true heir. The attempted resolution of this problem produces a competing heir. Due to Hagar's fleeing, Abram is in jeopardy of losing of who will later be the competing heir as well[10]

Sarai also blames Abram. Despite the fact that Sarai initiated the event, she refers to Hagar's pregnancy as wrong done to her, blaming Abram for it. Interestingly, the word she uses is *ḥamas* which means "violence" as well as "wrong". In turn her treatment of Hagar approaches violence. But in her frustration and anger, she still turns to the Lord, entreating him to determine who is in the wrong. In this we see her developing faith and trust in God.

We also see Abram having trust in God. He knows that God will give him a son, basing his belief on what God has told him in Gen 15:4. Sarah's solution appears to be God's answer to the dilemma he faces. His intense desire to have an heir blinds him to the true plan of God for him. Ironically when Hagar's son is born, Abram names him Ishmael (Gen 16:15), meaning "God hears". The choice of name further speaks to Abram's desperate longing for a son. God has finally heard his pleas. He now has an heir. But his "heir" is outside of God's plan. Eventually he will have to be sent away.

Reflection and Application ───────────────────────────────────────

God only has our best interests at heart. How often do we attempt to take matters into our own hands, as if we knew better? When we do so we often find ourselves experiencing more difficulty than what we were trying to resolve. "When we try to build something by ourselves, without God or outside of God, the result is always devastating."[11]   What things am I trying to build up on my own? When we attempt to build ourselves up without God we will fail. "Unless the Lord builds the house, they labor in vain who build it (Ps 127:1). Are we willing to depend on God for everything?

Notice also how in both the story of Sarai and Hagar and in that of Adam and Eve, blame is cast on another. Adam blames Eve for causing him to sin. Sarai blames Abram for impregnating Hagar (Gen 16:5) even though she was the one who came up with the idea. Our natural tendency is to refuse to take responsibility when we sin. It is so much easier to blame someone else. How often do I find myself doing the same? Who or what am I blaming for something that I ultimately caused?

It is very easy to become so fixated on something that we ignore everything around us. Like Abram, how often do my desires blind me to what God wants to accomplish through my life? Pray that God will open your eyes to see what he is doing.

THE CHANGE OF NAMES (GEN 17)

Like Genesis 15, chapter 17 contains another ratification of the covenant. In chapter 15 the description is one-sided, as Abram is asleep. Here it is two-sided, as Abram is to walk before God and be blameless. The hithpael verb form of the word "to walk" is reflexive as it is when God walks in the Garden of Eden (Gen 3:8). It suggests there being more of an intimate relationship between Abram and God than do the earlier passages. Both passages carry the sense of walking back and forth together.

No longer is he merely to have many descendants (Gen 15:5), but he will be the father of nations (Gen 17:4-6). Before he was just told to go (Gen 12:1-2). Now he is told to walk blamelessly, connected to the God who is blameless.

Reflection and Application ————————————————————————————

God desires for us to walk back and forth with him as well. Two of the best ways of doing this are through meditating on his Word and through prayer. These are ways we can draw closer to him. How would I describe my habits of prayer and meditating on his Word? What might God desire me to do differently?

The call to Abram is twenty four years in the past when God announces that he is changing Abram's and Sarai's names. It has been thirteen years since Ishmael was born. Abram becomes Abraham, Sarai becomes Sarah. What is the significance of the name change? As noted earlier, "Abram" means "exalted father". His name change includes the addition of one Hebrew letter in the middle of his name, the letter *hê*. The root word *r-m* "exalted" becomes *r-h-m* "multitude." "Abraham" means "father of multitudes." "Sarai" means "my princes" or "woman of strength", whereas "Sarah" means "princess of all." Why does God wait all these years to enact their name changes? Earlier they weren't ready to receive new names. God had to work on them, to bring healing to their lives before they were ready. Sarah had to become dependent on God before she could be a "princess of all" and the mother of nations (Gen 17:15-16).

We don't know what all happened during those thirteen years following Ishmael's birth, but we can guess what it must have been like for Sarah. She had to watch the bond between Abraham and Ishmael developing, knowing that he was not her son. She would have been unable to experience the joy Abraham had at finally having what he thought was the promised son. Her treatment of Hagar suggests she was not happy with the situation. We don't know how long her bitterness and pain continued during those long thirteen years. But she comes out healed. As she hears that she will have a son her disbelief is expressed in laughter, not in bitterness and pain. Yet in her laughter there are seeds of faith. Ps 113:9 is almost a commentary on Sarah.

For thirteen long years we have heard nothing of God's interaction with Abraham. He has been silent. Was this due to Abraham's lack of belief in God's word to him, instead siring a son with Hagar? We don't know, nor do we know whether Abraham felt a lack of God's presence in his life. When God does speak to him again he focuses on the covenant. The word "covenant" occurs ten times and the word "descendant" occurs six times in Genesis 17:1-14. As God speaks to him, Abraham thinks of Ishmael. When he hears that Sarah herself will have a son he still is thinking of Ishmael, saying "Oh that Ishmael might live before thee." (Gen 17:16-18). We might have expected to hear him say, "Finally, at last!" It is possible that part of Sarah's later insistence to send Ishmael away was due to Abraham's great devotion to him.

Abraham had to truly believe that God would really give him a son by Sarah, and later be willing to sacrifice his so longed-for only beloved son before he could become a "father of multitudes." But first, God had to bring healing to their lives. Sarah had to deal with the pain of childlessness and learn that God was not only Abram's God but her God as well. Abram had to believe that God would make him into a father of multitudes, although he would still be confused as to how this would come about. In Gen 17:18 he still wishes that his beloved Ishmael would be the chosen one. He still has to become convinced to do things God's way instead of his. This will be completed in the coming sacrifices of his sons.

Abram and Sarai's name changes have something almost prophetic about them. It is no longer just about Abraham and Sarah. While they are carriers of the divine blessing, the focus begins to change to the multitudes who will carry their name and through whom the blessing will continue to be realized. By changing his name to Abraham, God affirms the truthfulness of the covenant promise.

"We cannot do our part and fulfill the destiny that the Lord has prepared for each of us unless our heart is whole, unless we are reconciled fully to who we are and where we are. Before the circumstances change, and in order for them to change, an inner healing of the heart has to take place. We need to allow the Lord to transform the invisible first, and then the visible will be transformed as well."[12]

The naming of children by their parents today often has a significance as well. A family name may be chosen, or some sort of hope or dream is attached to it. When our second son was born, we named him Jonathan with the hope that he and his older brother David would be good friends. Many children are given biblical names for this reason.

CIRCUMCISION[13] (GEN 17:10-14, 23-27)

As part of the eternal covenant that God makes with Abraham, Abraham and his family are to be circumcised. Abraham circumcises himself and all the males of his household. After Abraham, Jewish infants would be circumcised on the eighth day (Gen 21:4). This rite will identify Jews as part of the covenantal family of God. It shows a separation between them and other people. It is intended to be both a physical and spiritual circumcision. In a spiritual sense it is to be a cutting away of the attractiveness of the world, a refusal to be like it. That separation is to be continual process.

Reflection and Application ─────────────────────────────────────

For the church, baptism is a type of circumcision. It identifies us as a member of the family of God. It is also to be both a physical and a spiritual rite. We are to remove "the foreskin of the world" with its selfish pleasures which block our ability to draw closer to God. Remembering our baptism is to remind us of the distinctiveness we have in Christ. What things do I need to cut out of my life that keep me from drawing closer to God?

A PLACE FOR ISHMAEL (GEN 17:15-21)

At God's call to Abraham in Gen 12:2 he is told a great nation will come from him. In Gen 15:4 this promise is further refined when God states that this will come about through Abraham's own son. Now it is even further refined by stating that the promised son will be Abraham and Sarah's son. Abraham thought he already had his son. For thirteen years he has been grooming Ishmael to be his successor. He wasn't expecting another son, nor did he really want one. He was content. But God now reveals his true plan. Abraham's request may indicate he wasn't exactly thrilled at the news, as he pleads with God "Oh that Ishmael might live before you." He effectively tells God "This is how I want things to be." God tells him that although he will bless Ishmael, Isaac will be the child to carry the covenant line forward.

Reflection and Application ——————————————————————————————

When things appear to be going in a certain direction it is easy to desire that they continue that way. Abraham did with Ishmael. Have there been times in my life when I thought things were going in a certain direction and found God changing my course in mid stream? Describe the situation.

ABRAHAM AND THE THREE VISITORS (GEN 18)

The events which take place in Genesis chapters 17 and 18 seem to have taken place very close together. At the news that Sarah will have a son, Abraham laughs. For this reason the Lord announces that his name will be Isaac, meaning "he laughs." One has the sense that Abraham hadn't yet communicated God's message about the coming birth of Isaac (Gen 17:15-17) to Sarah, as she seems surprised at the news in Gen 18:12. Abraham, still has hopes that Ishmael will be the chosen one (Gen 17:18). God makes it very clear that Isaac will be the chosen one.

One of the men who appears to Abraham, the spokesman for the group, is the Lord, possibly the pre-incarnate Christ. The chapter begins with the notice that the LORD appeared to him.

Abraham's generous hospitality is striking. Although hospitality was expected in their culture, it almost seems excessive. Abraham goes out of his way to be hospitable. There is nothing in the text to indicate that he saw this as an inconvenience. What Sarah thought might have been different! His action shows great care for his guests. The invitation to a meal doesn't occur because the three visitors show up just as they are about to eat; nothing is prepared. It would have taken a considerable number of hours to slaughter the calf, dress and cook it, and bake bread, all the while entertaining the visitors. A full meal is provided: meat, bread, milk, and curds.

Reflection and Application ───

Our hectic lives have a more difficult time with hospitality than Abraham's world did. With our full calendars and busy schedules it can seem to be an inconvenience, especially when the opportunity to be hospitable occurs in impromptu situations. It leads to the attitude of "I'll be hospitable when I have time for it." Unfortunately the time never seems to come. Hospitality is one of the gifts of the Holy Spirit that we should seek. It is also one of the keys of a loving heart. In what ways am I hospitable? How can I be more so?

Just like with Abraham and Sarah, God comes with a plan to help, comfort, and bless us in times of need. It is important for us to seek to see how he is working in our lives.

HOLY LAUGHTER (GEN 17:17; 18:9-15; 21:9-13)

In the culture of the day the women and children would have been in a separate part of the tent when strangers were entertained. With tent walls not being soundproof, Sarah would have heard the discussion the men were having. Upon hearing that she would have a child, she laughed. After waiting 24 years with no child, having passed menopause, it would seem impossible to continue to have hope. And so she laughed. It was a laugh of disbelief. But it is also a laugh of faith. God, as *El Shaddai*[14] (Gen 17:1), comes with a promise. Nothing is impossible with him. Sarah will definitely have a son in the coming year.

There is much more in these texts than we see at first glance. Laughter is the central motif in the story of Isaac's birth. Do we see more than one kind of laughter occurring in the story? How do we distinguish between Abraham's and Sarah's laughter? What about

Ishmael's laughter? When Abraham laughs God is silent, but when Sarah laughs God questions her about it. Why the difference? It is important to know the context of each to gain an understanding of what is going on. Abraham's laughter comes in the context of a direct revelation from God. His laughter is more of a "Oh my goodness! I can't believe it! I'm going to have a child!" It is a joyous laughter that is based on faith in what God has told him (Gen 17:16-17). The context behind Sarah's laughter is quite different. She doesn't have the direct revelation from God that Abraham has. All she knows is what she overheard three strange men who have accepted their hospitality telling Abraham. She doesn't know they are angels. She likely had not even seen them which might have given her a clue that they were more than mere mortals (Gen 18:9-10). Her laughter seems more cynical—a "really? Is this even possible?" God accuses her of a lack of faith in his ability to go above nature. Her proper response to the angel's message should have been an "Amen! May it be so!"—a prayer from her mouth to the ears of God who hears.

With all of the hurt she has felt in being barren all of these years she may have not even have been aware of inwardly laughing or may not have wanted to admit she had done so. It is interesting to note that God doesn't directly condemn her for laughing. He just points it out. He only points out what she has said about herself, omitting what she had said about Abraham. This shows the compassionate side of God.

Their son is appropriately named Isaac, which means "laughter." Through the background of Isaac's birth, Sarah becomes greatly sensitive to the nuances of laughter. It comes up again in the celebration of Isaac's weaning (Gen 21:8-9). While the English translations speak of Ishmael mocking or playing with Isaac, the Hebrew word is the participial form of the verb "to laugh." It appears he was expressing derisive laughter at Isaac. This may have led to Sarah's demand that he be sent away.

Reflection and Application ———————————————————————————————————

Real laughter is good for both the body and the soul. It releases endorphins in the body which promote well-being and reduce stress. Proverbs 17:22 reflects this fact. Psalms 126:1-2 points to the joy of laughter when the totally unexpected occurs. Laughter often occurs in the context of two extremes. In the midst of something progressing in a particular direction an extreme reversal occurs pointing in the other direction. The situation seems so amazing, so crazy, or absurd that the appropriate response is laughter. There is nothing more amazing or crazy than Abraham and Sarah having a child in their old age.

But at times the situation isn't funny at all, at which point it becomes inappropriate laughter. It can be our making a joke about something we want to do that we know is morally wrong. It allows us to feel more comfortable about doing it. It can be laughing at something which happened to someone else which we wouldn't want to have happen to us. In this way inappropriate laughter can become the starting point of immoral behavior. What is the nature of my laughter?

It is significant to note that despite her laughter, Sarah is noted to be a woman of faith (Heb 11:11). In many ways Sarah and Mary, as described in the Gospel of Luke are very similar. Both questioned "How is this even possible?" (Gen 18:12; Lu 1:34). Both stand out in their belief and trust in God.

THE SODOM DECISION (GEN 18:16-33)

The English texts of Gen 18:19 ("for I have chosen him" NASB; "for I have singled him out" NAB) don't quite capture the meaning of the Hebrew text which reads "for I have known him." It speaks of the relationship that God had with Abraham. It is because of their intimate relationship that Abraham will be able to bring up his children to keep God's ways, living in righteousness and justice. He knows God. Because of their relationship God deliberates, then decides to tell Abraham his plans regarding Sodom.

Although God doesn't say he will destroy Sodom, Abraham knows the heart of God. And so he pleads for Sodom, knowing that Lot and his family are there. He also knows Sodom, how evil it really is. He begins with a plea for sparing the city on behalf of fifty righteous, whittling it down to ten. It seems obvious that from the start Abraham doubts there are even fifty righteous individuals in Sodom. The statement in Gen 18:25 "Far be it from Thee to do such a thing" might be better translated "May it never be", similar to St Paul's statement in I Cor 6:15.[15] Abraham confronts God. Each time God accedes to Abraham's request. Abraham challenges God on behalf of the salvation of others. He pleads not just for the righteous to be spared, but for all of the inhabitants of the city. God called on Abraham and his family to act justly (Gen 18:19). Abraham turns the tables on God, pleading with him to also act justly (Gen 18:24-33).

His dialogue with God points to another spiritual truth. A minority of the righteous can have a profound effect upon a community. In this case a minority of ten righteous people would have spared Sodom from judgment.

The story ends with God remembering Abraham, and sparing Lot (Gen 19:29). In a similar vein, God remembers Noah and spares him (Gen 8:1). For God to remember in this way is to be mindful of those who are in relationship with him. Abraham is certainly one of them.

Reflection and Application ————————————————————————————

Abraham was willing to take the risk of divine displeasure in challenging and questioning God. It is important to note that he does so in humility. He speaks of himself as being dust and ashes (Gen 18:27). In this he connects himself with Adam and creation. He could be bold in pleading with God in prayer because he had an intimate relationship with him. God knew him and he knew God. We are called to know God, but he first knows us. Am I as known by God as Abraham was? Do I have such an intimate relationship with God, as Abraham did, so I can know his heart? Ask God for help in knowing him better, through the study of his word and through prayer. Make a concerted effort to know him better.

It is OK to question God as long as it is done with humility. It is an admission that we don't have all the answers and are confused by what we see God doing.

It is important to always pray that righteousness will be manifest in the community in which we live. Whatever political party one affiliates with, he should always pray that the leaders of the party in power will lead with righteousness and judgment. To what extent do I do this?

Because much is made of Abraham's dialogue with God in this section, there is something often overlooked in verses 17–19. God says he chose Abraham to command his children and his household after him to keep the way of God in righteousness and justice. He says this is necessary for him to bless Abraham. As we continue our way through Genesis we will see this working out through Abraham's family and descendants. Abraham instructs

Isaac, who instructs Jacob, who instructs his sons. When Moses speaks to the Israelites in Deuteronomy, he tells them that the message he is giving them must be taught to their children (Deut 6:6-9). While nothing is mentioned in the story of the patriarchs of their teaching their children, they must have done so, for their children also followed the Lord. We see them continuing to grow in faith.

Reflection and Application ———————————————————————————————

God's mention of the importance of Abraham teaching his children is a good lesson for us as well. The best way of passing on the faith is by teaching and living it. As we continue on through Genesis, we will see how Abraham lived out his faith. Isaac caught it. We see him meditating with the Lord (Gen 24:63). Am I teaching the faith to my children? More importantly, am I living out my faith where my children can see it?

ABRAHAM AT GERAR (GEN 20)

One would have thought that Abraham would have learned that God would provide for him during his sojourn in Egypt. Apparently he didn't because he again passes off Sarah, now likely pregnant, as his sister. It comes out that she actually is both his wife and step sister (Gen 20:12). While calling Sarah his sister was technically true, it was a deceptive truth. Abraham has the same fear of being killed (Gen 20:11) as he had in Egypt.

Reflection and Application ———————————————————————————————

The story reminds us that while it is possible to have tremendous faith, we are still human. We will fail. Confession and absolution restores us and allows us to get back up and begin again.

Truth is important. It can be easy to give only the partial truth that places us in good light. Partial truth often leads to the sin of deception. It is better to say nothing than to speak only partial truth.

THE BIRTH OF ISAAC AND BANISHMENT OF ISHMAEL (GEN 21)

It becomes clear to Abraham and Sarah that it is God who has given them a son. Gen 21:1 states that "the LORD did for Sarah as he promised." Isaac, being weaned, may be about two years old, making Ishmael around sixteen. The text makes it clear that Abraham still greatly loved his older son. When the birth of Isaac had been foretold, he pleaded with God, "Oh that Ishmael might live before thee!" (Gen 17:18). When Sarah now confronts Abraham, telling him to drive Hagar and Ishmael away, Abraham is grievously distressed. How can he send his beloved son away? This is perhaps the only time we visibly see Abraham's emotions (Gen 21:11). God tells him to listen to Sarah because it is through Isaac, not Ishmael, that his descendants will be named. Abraham does as God commands. With pain in his heart, he sends Ishmael and Hagar away, giving them some bread and a skin of water. In his heart he must have felt that he was sending them out into the desert wilderness to die, even though God said he would make of Ishmael a nation also. He could only trust that God would be true to his word.

What led to this family breakup? It doesn't seem likely that it is due to Ishmael having a bad attitude towards Isaac. Had it been that, the breakup would have occurred before Isaac was a toddler. The Hebrew text of Gen 21:9 gives a clue, though not in the English translations. Various words are used to describe what Ishmael was doing which made Sarah so upset. The NASB translates it "mocking", NAB "playing", ESV "laughing" with a footnote calling it mocking laughter, etc. The Hebrew word is the participle form of the verb that Isaac's name is from, meaning "laughter." Why would Ishmael's laughter be so upsetting? The answer is found in Sarah's rant to Abraham about Ishmael not being an heir. The name Isaac means "he laughs." Ishmael, in laughing, draws upon the meaning of Isaac's name, in effect claiming to be the heir of the promise as well.[16]

Abraham is displeased with sending Ishmael away. But he sends him away out of obedience to God's directive. By sending him out into the harsh desert wilderness he was effectively imposing a death sentence upon him.

Although Ishmael is not the chosen son, God still provides for him and blesses him, promising that he will be the father of a great nation (Gen 21:18-20). We don't know his feelings at being cast out, but he must have experienced envy and jealousy. After all, for fourteen years he had been the privileged son. He doesn't know the pain and suffering the chosen son is about to face on Mount Moriah.

Reflection and Application ———————————————————————

God tells Abraham that he should accept Sarah's counsel. How many times have we had difficulties because we have not listened to the words of our spouse? Often they have God-given wisdom we need to hear and follow.

THE ROLE OF ELECTION

It is often felt that when the Bible speaks of someone being elected, others are excluded. Therefore, Isaac is elected and Ishmael is excluded. But when we look at the text of Genesis 17 and 21 we see something different. When Abraham asks that God would remember Ishmael God says that he will bless Ishmael and make his descendants into a great nation. Hagar is told the same in Gen 21:17-18. Ishmael receives much the same sort of blessing as Isaac does. The major difference is that Isaac receives the promise as the chosen one. This topic will be dwelt on again in the discussion of Jacob and Esau.

THE SACRIFICE OF ISAAC (GEN 22)[17]

For most of his life Abraham had longed for a son. Late in life he was finally blessed with two sons. Then God called him to effectively sacrifice his elder son by sending him out into the desert wilderness where he would only continue to live by the grace of God. At the beginning of his call God told him to *lech lecha*—"go to yourself" (Gen 12:1). Now he tells him *lech lecha* again (Gen 22:2). Now God asks him to sacrifice his only remaining son. Just as he had to leave behind his desires, his baggage, and his cultural understandings, he now has to do so all over again.

We usually think of Isaac as still being a child when this took place. If Sarah's death is tied to this incident, Isaac could have been much older. Jewish tradition considers him to be about 37 years old at this time.[18] Abraham has a dilemma. What was he to do? To sacrifice Isaac would certainly lead to his death. Again we see his great faith in his obedience to the call of God. In the Old Testament there are five men who are considered to be great men of faith. They are Abraham, Jacob, Moses, Samuel and Isaiah. Each of the five was called by God to serve him. Each responded in exactly the same way. They responded "hineni." The Hebrew word *hineni* means "Here am I." But it has a deeper meaning. It means not only am I listening, but I am also ready to carry out your command. This is the point where Abraham finally places total trust in God. He doesn't question, he doesn't flinch. He starts on the journey to carry out God's command.

In actuality there are two sacrifices and two salvations in Genesis 21 and 22, both Ishmael and Isaac. The Hebrew text bears this out by using the same words in both accounts. In both accounts the **angel of the LORD calls from heaven** (Gen 21:17; 22:11). In Gen 21:18 Hagar is told to take Ishmael's **hand**; in Gen 22:12 Abraham is told not to use his **hand** against Isaac. Hagar's **eyes were opened and she saw** a well of water (Gen 21:19); Abraham's **eyes were opened and he saw** a ram (Gen 22:13). Both Ishmael and Isaac were at the point of death when their lives were spared (Gen 21:16; 22:10).

The commonality between these two accounts points to the grace of God. Both have been sacrificed. Both have been redeemed. Both Ishmael and Isaac experience God's saving grace, though only one of them is the chosen son.

Abraham names the place "The Lord will see" (Gen 22:14). It is interesting that the verb is future instead of "has seen". There may be a prophetic sense to his choice of the verb form. It is on Mount Moriah that the temple was built and it is close to where God looked down on his son hanging on a cross, and turned away (Mk 15:34).

In the book of Revelation Christ is acclaimed as the lamb who was slain (Rev 5:12). He is elsewhere identified as the lamb only by the testimony of John the Baptist in John 1:29, 36. Since the word "lamb" seldom occurs in the Old Testament, one can wonder where he picked up the concept of the Messiah being the Lamb of God. The answer may be found in the sacrifice of Isaac (called the *Akedah* or *Binding of Isaac* in Jewish literature). The first occurrence of the word lamb in the Bible occurs in Isaac's question to his father: "Behold the fire and the wood, but where is the lamb?" (Gen 22:7-8). Abraham responds that God will provide the lamb. It is interesting to note that rabbinic literature considered Isaac to have been slain and brought back to life, with Abraham responding to Isaac, "You are the lamb, my son."[19] Isaac was viewed as being a willing sacrifice. This makes more sense if he was an adult. During the 150–year period before Christ, Jewish theology began to view the sacrifice of Isaac as atoning for Israel's sins. With this in mind it is easy to see why John calls Jesus "the lamb of God."[20] Isaac prefigures Christ as a willing sacrifice.

Reflection and Application

Earlier we said that faith involves taking risks. Abraham takes the greatest risk of all when he sacrifices his son. In obedience to God he risks the death of his son. He sent one son away to die unless God intervened. He may not have known whether Ishmael was alive or not. Now he is about to kill what might be his only surviving son, the one God had promised would carry his name. In total faith, as the knife began its downward stroke, he must have believed that if he killed Isaac God would bring him back to life.

There are times when we are all called upon to sacrifice something. It may be something that we really like to do, a particular job, something we need to give up, etc. Most of us aren't called upon to sacrifice our lives as modern–day martyrs have done. Is there anything God is asking me to sacrifice at this point in my life? What hinders me from doing so?

At various points in our lives God calls us to serve him in some way. What is my response when he calls? Do I, like the Old Testament saints, respond "Hineni" and step forward in faith?

EXCURSUS: THE BIBLICAL DOCTRINE OF ATONEMENT

The doctrine of atonement is often discussed in theology. The word can be divided as "at-one-ment" with the meaning of "bringing those who are estranged into a unity." Atonement is necessary because of sin, its seriousness, and our inability to deal with it.[21] The word occurs six times in the Bible.[22] Leviticus 23:27-28 gives instructions about the annual day of atonement. The need for atonement was well known in Jewish thought. Around 150 years before Christ, Jewish rabbis began to connect atonement with the *Aqedah* (sacrifice) of Isaac, holding that Abraham sacrificed both Isaac and the ram. Isaac, as a willing innocent sacrifice shedding his blood, was viewed as an atonement. It was held that when David ordered the census, what God saw that caused him to stop the plague against David was the atoning sacrifice of Isaac (I Chron 21:15).

Between around 150 BC through the beginning of the Christian era, Jewish scholars began to establish the belief that atonement for the sins of Israel came from Isaac's self sacrifice and shedding of his blood. This Aqedah, with its free sacrifice was considered above all others, with benefits for all time.[23]

In this view, when Abraham said "you are the lamb" he totally meant it! The apocryphal book of 4 Maccabees dated to the middle of the first century AD points to the belief of Isaac's sacrifice when it says "He read to you about Abel slain by Cain, and Isaac who was offered as a burnt offering, and of Joseph in prison." (4 Macc 18:11)

In this regard Isaac becomes a type of Christ. The New Testament writers use the concept of atonement in speaking of what Christ has done for us–(cf. Rom 3:25; Heb 2:17; I Jn 2:2; 4:10). While Isaac is seen in Jewish eyes as offering atonement for Israel, Jesus, the greater Isaac, offers atonement for the entire world.

ISAAC AS A TYPE OF CHRIST[24]

There are several parallels between Jesus and Isaac. The annunciation of their births are comparable. Both are given by angels (Gen 18:10-15; Luke 1:26-35). Both are received with incredulity. Sarah is past child bearing age and Mary is a virgin. Neither are in a position to have a child. Both Isaac and Jesus are given names before their birth (Gen 17:19; Lu 1:31). We only have brief hints about their early years. Abraham is called to sacrifice "his only son" (Gen 22:2) and God gives "his only begotten son" (Jn 3:16). Abraham and Isaac go on a three day journey to make the sacrifice (Gen 22:4). Jesus was in the tomb for three days. The wood is placed on Isaac's shoulder (Gen 22:6) and Jesus carries the wood of his cross (Jn 19:17). Jerusalem was built on Mount Moriah, so both could have been sacrificed at, or close to, the same place. Both sons are obedient to their fathers. If Jewish scholars are right, both may have been close to the same age at the time of their sacrifices. Some Jewish rabbis believe that Isaac was actually sacrificed and raised from the dead[25], as was Jesus.

Hebrews 11:18 indicates that however Isaac's sacrifice exactly happened, Abraham firmly believed that God could raise Isaac from the dead. Abraham's seeing the ram just in the nick of time is a sort of raising from the dead.

THE DISAPPEARANCE OF ISAAC (GEN 22:19)

Following what must have been a terrible shock at Mount Moriah Isaac disappears from the story, to reappear only when he meets Rebekah, likely three years later (Cf. "The death of Sarah" below). Abraham returns to the servants that had come with them, but Isaac doesn't (Gen 22:19). He doesn't appear in the story of his mother's death. This may explain why her death upset him so much (Gen 24:67). Where is he? Abraham returns to live at Beersheba while Isaac is later reported to have been living separately in the Negev (Gen 24:62). It is significant that he had been at Beer-lahai-roi, which means "The One Who Sees Me Lives". This is where Hagar met the angel (Gen 16:7-14). It is likely that Hagar and Ishmael went to Beer-lahai-roi after their banishment. Isaac's being there may indicate he went there to be reconciled with his brother.[26] While Isaac may have disappeared from human sight, he was still in God's sight. That he was meditating may indicate a developing closeness with God following the Moriah experience. If so, this was a time of spiritual retreat for him.

Reflection and Application

There are times in our lives when we need to get away to draw close to God. St Paul did this during his time in Arabia (Gal 1:17). These can be times of renewal, times of receiving guidance, or merely times of drawing closer to our Lord. Such times can be especially beneficial after we have gone through difficult times.

THE RENEWAL OF THE PROMISE (GEN 22:15-18)

After Abraham's sacrifice of Isaac God once again reaffirms the covenantal promise he had given to Abraham. God swears by himself that Abraham's progeny will be as many as the stars of heaven and the sands of the seashore. They will possess the gates of their enemies and be a blessing to the entire world. At the end of verse 18 God explains why. It wasn't because of Abraham's great faith for which he is known. Instead, it is because of his obedience. James 2:21-22 notes that Abraham was justified by his works. His faith was demonstrated by his works.

Faithfulness and obedience go hand in hand in the Bible. Obedience is evidence of faith. The relationship between faith and works is similar. Works give evidence of the faith we claim. James 2:14-26 is a commentary on the interplay between faith and works. A good question to ask from time to time is "What evidence in my life shows that I have faith?"

THE DEATH OF SARAH (GEN 23)

In Jewish tradition the account of the death of Sarah is juxtaposed with the account of Isaac's sacrifice. According to the Jewish commentary Rabbah 58,5 when she heard the news of the intended sacrifice of her son, her soul left her and she died. Effectively the shock on this elderly woman was too much for her. Since she was 127 years old, and Isaac was born when she was 90, he would have been 37 years old, if this suggestion is correct. The text notes that Abraham wept at Sarah's death (Gen 23:2). This is the first account of anyone weeping in the Bible. Hebrew manuscripts have a smaller letter *kapf* in the word translated "wept over". In Jewish circles it is thought that it indicates something about Abraham's emotional state. His grief was a controlled grief. While deeply upset he did not despair, knowing that somehow God was in this.[27]

There is something else of interest in the account–the interaction between Abraham and the sons of Heth. Abraham again shows his humble nature, calling himself merely a stranger and sojourner in their land, although God has promised it to him. They, on the other hand, refer to him as a mighty prince (Gen 23:4-6). They see more in him than he sees in himself.

Reflection and Application ⸻

It is always better for us to have a lesser attitude towards ourselves than others do. Jesus indicated this in the parable of the marriage feast (Lu 14:7-11). This helps us avoid pride. It also allows God to work through us. Others can see God's strength coming out of our weakness. We are to be channels of his blessing, not of our own.

Death is not intended to be normal. It is one of the consequences of the Fall. Grief is the natural response. According the Isaiah 53:3 the Suffering Servant was a "man of sorrows, acquainted with grief." Yet at the same time death is not the end. We have a hope for the future–Resurrection!

ABRAHAM'S CHARGE FOR FINDING ISAAC'S WIFE (GEN 24)

Abraham's decision to find a wife from his father's extended family doesn't seem to have been for religious reasons. Their family continued to have a polytheistic background which is still evident when Jacob flees from Laban many years later (Gen 31:19). Abraham's decision seems to be ethnically based. In any case, he desired Isaac to have a good wife. Abraham's charge to his servant shows us his faith. He has absolutely no doubt that his servant will be successful. God will guide him. The servant's response to Abraham's charge is more interesting as it informs us more about Abraham's faith. He has shared his faith with his household. His faith is not merely something private, but is something communicated. His servant is well aware of the nature of Abraham's faith in God. As he arrives at Haran he prays to God for success in finding a wife. This is the first occurrence of anyone in the Bible seeking divine guidance. Although he refers to Abraham's God, his words indicate he himself also has a relationship with God. He addresses a specific prayer to God (Gen 24:12-14), praises God for his guidance (Gen 24:27), and worships him (Gen 24:48). He has caught Abraham's faith and made it his own.

As we turn from Abraham to Isaac, note that the Bible says that Isaac loved his wife (Gen 24:67). This is the first of only two occurrences in the Bible describing the relationship between a man and his wife as one of love.

Reflection and Application

Faith is never meant to be only a private affair. It is meant to be communicated and communal. Abraham's faith was infectious. He shared it with his household—not only with Sarah and Isaac, but also with his servants and retainers. He also lived it, that others might live it as well. Do I do the same? Do I live and share my faith that others may see it in action?

The servant seeks God's guidance, believing that God will definitely point out the young woman who will become Isaac's wife (Gen 24:14). How often do I seek God's guidance in important decisions which must be made?

What kind of spouse do I want for my children? If I were to choose their spouse what would I focus on? Would it be their looks or social status? Or would it be their faith and their character? How can I teach my children what things are important in seeking a spouse?

THE CHOOSING OF REBEKAH (GEN 24:10-27)

There is much we can learn from this section. Abraham's servant decides to use an oracular approach to resolve the issue of who should be the chosen wife for Isaac. He seeks from God a yes / no decision to the problem, based on his question to the young woman. His test of the woman with respect to watering his camels would have been outside of the realm of possibility. It would have taken hours. No one would have volunteered to water the camels unless God intervened.[28] That Rebekah volunteered for the task confirmed in his mind that she was the one.

The servant doesn't seek a young woman of beauty or wealth, although he finds one who is beautiful. Instead he seeks a woman of good character, one with a kind, serving, and humble heart. When he meets her family he gives an eloquent testimony to the work of God on his behalf. Bethuel and Laban, although not followers of God, recognize this and give their permission for the marriage (Gen 24:50-51).

Reflection and Application

The method the servant used is similar to the fleece method used by Gideon to determine whether God was really calling him to lead Israel (Jud 6:36-40). As time goes on this method is used less and less, replaced by words from the prophets. After Christ we have the leading of the Holy Spirit in our lives. While God can definitely use circumstances to lead us, this method has two dangers. The first is that it effectively is an attempt to force God to act as we dictate, with a yes or no response. The second is that history has shown it to be an unreliable method. The medieval test of water dunking, continuing up into the seventeenth century, where a person was either thrown into a river or dunked under water to determine innocence or guilt (with the rare survival indicating innocence) expected guilt and the majority died. Some people have equated healing from serious disease with God's favor, concluding that when he doesn't heal, there must be something wrong with them or that he is angry with them. While it can at times be the case, it can never be taken as a definite conclusion.

How do I respond when seeing people in need? Do I even notice them? Am I willing to extend my time and effort to help as Rebekah did?

Our society embraces status, beauty, and wealth. None of them has anything to do with character. Character is much more important, for it speaks volumes about the person. For a young person, seeking a marriage partner, character and faith are the most important things to focus on.

THE DEATH OF ABRAHAM (GEN 25)

Since Abraham sends all his other children away, it is easy to overlook the importance of Isaac and Ishmael being together to bury their father. God is a God of relationships. He desires his children to be in relationship as well. The importance of relationships will come up again in the stories of Jacob and Joseph.

THE TESTS OF ABRAHAM

Throughout Abraham's life he is tested many times. The tests and challenges he faced are listed below.

1. The call to leave his land
    God calls him to step out and leave everything he knew behind. He was to leave his land, his relatives, his inheritance, and his family to go to an uncertain place with an uncertain future.
2. Escaping the famine
    God had promised to give him the land of Canaan. It was for him and his descendants. Now he leaves this land in order to survive. Since God didn't tell him to go, was this a failed test or not?
3. The injustice of the Egyptians towards Sarah
    Sarah is taken into the court of Pharaoh as a concubine, seeming to void the promise of Sarah as the mother of Abraham's children.
4. War with the four kings
    Abraham, with his retainers, marches 500 plus miles to rescue Lot, defeating a far superior military force.

5. Taking Hagar as a wife

   His willingness to take Hagar as a wife seems one test that he failed, unwilling to wait on God's timing.

6. Rite of circumcision

   Performing the painful rite of circumcision on himself, family, and servants at age 99

7. Injustice of the king of Gerer

   He also took Sarah, seeming to void the promise of Sarah as the mother of Abraham's children.

8. Expulsion of Hagar and Ishmael

   After 13 years of loving Ishmael and thinking of him as his heir, Abraham is told to send him away.

9. Sacrifice of Isaac

   This was the ultimate sacrifice, as there was nothing to gain and everything to lose. It also led to a possible estrangement with Isaac.

Why was he tested? God obviously knew how the tests would turn out. What value did they have and why this ultimate final test? They had no benefit for God; but were significant in Abraham's life. In all but the last test Abraham had something to gain. They all involved something that brings self-satisfaction, whether he passed them or not. Going to Canaan meant gaining land, going to Egypt meant food, Sarah's abduction ended up meaning gifts, etc. The last test is about self-sacrifice. There is no benefit to Abraham in Isaac's death. It is just the opposite. Everything he had worked for and God had promised would be wasted. As we look at this final test we see that ultimately they were all about the same thing. They are all about God, with Abraham not thinking of himself at all.

The Hebrew word *nisa* (test) is related to two other Hebrew words. One means "banner or pole,"; the other "miracle." When a person goes through testing it often brings out a kind of miracle. Latent potential comes forward as untapped abilities and fortitude exhibit themselves as the person rises to the occasion. They see how God enables them to survive the test, and their faith is enhanced. Passing the test serves as a banner to others, giving them encouragement as they experience their own tests. As Abraham went through these tests and saw God working in his life, when the ultimate test to sacrifice his son came, he readily said "Here am I, ready to go."

Reflection and Application ———————————————————————————————————

We all go through tests and challenges as times. While we pray in the Lord's Prayer "Lead us not into temptation, but deliver us from evil," when tests come we should welcome them as opportunities to grow in our faith. How have the tests I have gone through in the past increased my faith? Are there any tests I am currently facing?

The tests which Abraham faced are the same ones we face, and come to us in the same manner they came to Abraham. By the end, Abraham was a totally God-centered person. Will I also be God-centered, or will I be self-centered or ego-centered? How I answer this question has eternal consequences.

CHAPTER 2

Isaac and Rebekah

ISAAC AS A CHILD (GEN 22)

In many ways the story of Isaac serves as a bridge between Abraham and Jacob. The story of Abraham covers thirteen chapters in Genesis. That of Jacob covers twenty-three chapters. The story of Isaac is very much abbreviated, covering only three chapters. Even though it is very short, there is much we can learn.

We are not told what Isaac's emotional state was like after the attempted sacrifice. Was he emotionally scarred for life? Was it a moment when faith became real as he saw God providing a ram for the sacrifice at the last moment? Did Isaac also hear the message of the angel to Abraham? Or as the rabbinical tradition holds, was he killed and brought back to life? We can also wonder how this event affected his relationship with his father. While we can imagine Abraham saying to Isaac on the return trip from Mount Moriah, "Now don't say anything about this to your mother!" we don't know what effect it had. Other than the brief mention of him when Abraham sends his servant to find a wife for Isaac, the next we hear of him is when he meets Rebekah (Gen 24:62-67). The text indicates that it may have brought him closer to his mother, for he is distraught after her death, to be comforted only when he brings Rebekah to her tent after three years grieving her death (Gen 24:67).

As mentioned earlier, Isaac totally disappeared after the scene at Mount Moriah, with the suggestion that these years were a time of spiritual renewal for him. That he is the only one of the Patriarchs who doesn't have a name change supports this. Abram becomes Abraham. Jacob becomes Israel. Isaac stays Isaac.

THE YOUNG REBEKAH (GEN 24:15-67)

Of all the Patriarchal women, Rebekah receives the most detail. Much more ink is used to describe her compared to either Sarah or Rachel. Her action at the well points out aspects of her character. It is an act of kindness. It shows her having a servant's heart, willing to help others, even strangers in their need. She needs no prompting to water the animals. She observes the need and acts upon it. She has the exact qualities Abraham's servant is looking for. We see her faith in action when asked if she will consent to marry Isaac. She had never met Isaac and knew nothing about him. She based her decision solely on what she had heard. She has heard the explanation of Abraham's servant when he told of how God had guided him. Although from a polytheistic family her response is an immediate trusting "Yes" (Gen 24:57-58). In this she makes a similar choice to the one made by Abram many years before, to step out in faith and go to an unknown land at the urging of God.

The English translations don't do justice to Rebekah's meeting Isaac. Gen 24:64 literally says that she "fell off her camel." Jewish Rabbis held that one result of Isaac's time alone with God was his face was shining much as Moses' face had (Ex 34:29). The Rabbinic commentator Rashi reflecting on this passage says, "When the heart humbles itself before God in the fire of testing, it is cleansed and filled with God's glory. Isaac is coming up out of the desert, radiating God's light."[29] Rebekah also veiled herself (Gen 24:65). Whether this was merely for modesty or because of Isaac's visage is uncertain.

Whether or not Rashi's comment is true, it contains a great lesson. A humble heart filled with the glory of God is an awesome thing. We are to humbly radiate God's light to the world, to reflect the light of Christ. What sort of heart do I have? When others look at me do they see Christ?

ISAAC AS A LOVING MAN OF PRAYER (GEN 24: 62-63 AND 25:21)

The text says Isaac loved Rebekah. Of the three patriarchs only Isaac is said to love his wife. We see evidence of this in his praying for her. Like Sarah before and Rachel after her, Rebekah struggled with infertility. By the time she finally becomes pregnant nineteen years have passed. Abraham only complains to God about Sarah's infertility; there is no mention of his praying about it. When Rachel complains to Jacob about her infertility, he becomes angry with her, asking "Am I in the place of God?" (Gen 30:2). Isaac is the only one who prays for his wife. And God answers. Rebekah becomes pregnant, giving birth to the twins Esau and Jacob (Gen 25:25-26). Of the three Patriarchs, only Isaac is monogamous. Rebekah is his only wife through his long 180-year life.

The English translations of Gen 25:21 explain the interchange between Isaac and God, but miss a point contained in the Hebrew text. Most translations say that Isaac *prayed* and the Lord *answered*. That is what happened. The same Hebrew word is used in both cases. Isaac entreated God, and God entreated (or granted entreaty) back. Using the same word suggests a greater level of intimacy between Isaac and God.[30]

Isaac is also a man who spent time with God. He had gone to Beer-lahai-roi which means "the living one who sees me" in order to meditate. He demonstrated a practice of spending time with God (Gen 24:63). He is at prayer when he first sees Rebekah.

The place name Beer-lahai-roi is significant. It speaks to Isaac's relationship with God. The God who for all appearances turned his back on Isaac at Mount Moriah actually sees and knows him. We can well imagine that Isaac gave the place its name.

Reflection and Application ————————————————————

Prayer is an act of love, especially when for one's family. Too often we take our spouses for granted. How often do I pray for my spouse? If you haven't been, this is a good time to start.

How much time do I spend in God's presence? Do I spend time in meditating on his Word? If not as much as you feel God would have you, confess it and ask for his help.

THE REPEATED SISTER ACT (GEN 26:1-11)

We don't know whether Abraham told Isaac about his indiscretion in Egypt as he taught him about God's dealing with him. Since Isaac does the same it appears that he didn't. As with Abraham we see that lessons of faith are not easy. God has just told him to stay in the land of Canaan during the famine, that he would bless Isaac and be with him and his descendants (Gen 26:3-4). Isaac believes him and obeys. But he immediately fears for his life as his father had before him. What happened to his faith?

Abimelech's response when he learns of Isaac's duplicity is instructive. It points to the interconnectedness between individual and corporate responsibility. He says in verse 10 that one person's potential sin would have affected the entire community. The defeat at Ai due to Achan's sin in Joshua 7 reminds us of that principle.

Reflection and Application ───

As we look at the success and failures in both Abraham's and Isaac's faith one lesson stands out. Faith is not something that we are zapped with, so that we either we have it or we don't. Faith is something that grows over time. As we go through the experiences of life we learn to trust God more and more. It has been said that when we go through difficulties to remember God's history with us, seeing how he has been with us in the past, giving us more trust in his leading in the present situation and on into the future. What blessings has God given me in the past that I can look back on?

In our modern world we have a tendency to believe that sin is OK as long as it doesn't affect someone else. But that rarely is the case. We live in community. We sin in the midst of community. It affects the community and damages our relationship with God and others. Are there sins I have committed which have affected others or my community?

ISAAC THE PEACEMAKER (GEN 26:18-33)

Like Abraham before him, Isaac seeks to be a man of peace. When contention develops regarding the ownership of the wells, Isaac refuses to make an issue over them, instead moving and digging new wells. He also made a covenant of peace with Abimelech.

Reflection and Application ───────────────────────────────

Am I known as a person of peace? Am I a peacemaker or am I known as a contentious person? Must I always have things go my way? Jesus says in the Beatitudes "Blessed are the peacemakers." May we be known as such!

REBEKAH'S INQUIRY OF THE LORD (GEN 25:22-23)

The text suggests that Rebekah's pregnancy was very difficult. As a result she inquires of the Lord. Of all of the individuals in the Bible who inquired of the Lord, Rebekah is the only woman mentioned. In this she is in the company of Manoah, David, Jehoshaphat, and the Israelites as a nation. To inquire of God in the midst of her adversity speaks volumes to her faith, especially coming from a family that was polytheistic.[31] God responds to her prayer, stating that she would have twins.

God told her that the two babies represented two nations who would separate and go separate ways. One would be stronger than the other. The English texts make an interpretive leap in the last line of verse 23, stating "And the older shall serve the younger." This interpretation has Esau serving Jacob. The Hebrew text is more ambiguous. There are no definite articles with either noun which would indicate the subject. It could just as well mean "the younger shall serve the older". It is translated based on word order and the fact that the verb form is not passive. Also, the word translated "older" doesn't mean older. It means "many, great" lending itself to the translation "many shall serve the younger". This translation falls in line with the passages in Isaiah that speak of all nations coming to Jerusalem (Isa 55:5; 60:3, 5, 11, 16; 61:6; 66:20).

What is my response to adversity? Do I seek God's help? Is my first response to seek out what God might desire to teach me through the situation?

PARENTAL FAVORITISM (GEN 25:24-34)

We can wonder why Isaac gravitated towards Esau and Rebekah towards Jacob. The answer is found in the characters of the parents and of the children. Isaac was born in the land of Canaan and lived there all his life. Unlike his father who would have been considered a rancher, Isaac became a farmer as well, growing crops (Gen 26:12-14). He was tied to nature, enjoying the outdoors. Rebekah, on the other hand, came from an immigrant culture and background. She spent her time "in the tent" (Gen 24:67). The text indicates that both Isaac and Esau were outdoors type people. Isaac's place of meditation was out in the field (Gen 24:63). Esau is described as a "man of the field" (Gen 25:27). Both appear to have enjoyed hunting for wild game. Because of this Esau had a special place in Isaac's heart (Gen 25:28). Isaac's preference for Esau appears to be an obstacle to the divine plan given to Rebekah. Jacob, on the other hand, spent most of his time in more domestic activities (Gen 25:27). He didn't have the same relationship with his father that Esau had. His preferences brought him closer to his mother. God's revelation that the elder would serve the younger likely influenced her as well. There is no indication that Isaac or Rebekah didn't love the other son. While they loved both, it was obvious to anyone witnessing the family dynamics that each parent had a special bond with one of their children.

We can almost see in Isaac's and Rebekah's preferences an attempt to mold their favored son into the person of their own making. Were they each attempting to dictate what their favored child would become? We don't know whether parental favoritism caused the enmity which developed between the two brothers; it likely did since it is recorded as a significant point.

Esau and Jacob had very different personalities, as did their parents. We often find the same with ourselves and our children. Each child is different. At times it is easy to ask "How can these two children have the same parents? They are so different!" Yet it is important to love each equally. As we will see, the nature of the relationships Isaac and Rebekah had with their children would lead to difficulties in their children's lives.

We have all seen or heard of examples of parents dictating the lives of their children. Some choose the career path their son or daughter will take, or the school they will attend. Their child's desires are not considered. This often leads to resentment and a breakdown in family relationships. It certainly seems that this happened to Jacob and Esau.

The favoritism shown by Abraham for Ishmael and Isaac for Esau points to a danger we can experience; neither seemed aware that God knew what was best for them and was moving to see that it came to fruition. They became blind to what God was doing. How often do we do the same?

THE YOUNG JACOB AND ESAU (GEN 25:27-29)

As the two boys grow up it becomes increasingly clear that they are very different from each other. In today's verbiage we might say that Esau was athletic while Jacob was bookish. We don't know how early Rebekah saw the differences manifesting themselves or how much the prophecy she received affected her relationship with her sons. We only have hints at why they were at odds against each other, such as Jacob's stealing Esau's birthright (Gen 25:31-33). How much their character differences played into this is unknown. Was parental favoritism a factor? We don't know. But the enmity between the brothers defined and affected much of Jacob's life. We will see this again and again, beginning with his flight from Esau and his reconciliation with him twenty-some years later.

THE PROBLEM OF ESAU (GEN 25:27-34)

It is uncertain what the derivation of Esau's name is from. Given his color at birth it could be from *admoni* (reddish) or *dam* (blood). It could also be related to the word *asah* (making or doing). He becomes the ancestor of the Edomites who lived in what is now modern Jordan.

The struggle that begins in the womb continues throughout their lives. As they grow it becomes apparent that the two boys are much different from each other. Esau is an outdoors person who enjoys hunting. Jacob, on the other hand, has a domestic temperament. Esau seems to be impulsive, Jacob more scheming. Esau seems almost narcissistic in this text, thinking only of himself. He has difficulties dealing with delayed gratification (Gen 25:30–33). This makes him willing to abandon his birthright. The author, in telling the story, makes an editorial comment in Gen 25:34, noting that Esau despised his birthright. Esau becomes angry with Jacob for stealing his blessing, seeking to kill him. Their relationship, never completely harmonious is broken. Esau is in danger of becoming like Cain who killed his brother.

Reflection and Application

Many in our society have issues with narcissism and delayed gratification. We want things, and we want them now! Advertizing and the media focus on the now, saying we can have it all. The refusal to delay gratification often causes problems. It cost Esau his birthright. Are there issues in my life where I have refused to delay gratification? What problems did they cause?

But by the time Jacob returns to Canaan some twenty years later he is a changed man. He takes the initiative to restore the broken relationship with his brother (Gen 33:4). He runs to meet him, which given the culture was unlikely. He embraces him, kissing him and weeping. When Jacob attempts to offer restitution for stealing the blessing, Esau defers, saying that he has plenty, needing nothing more (Gen 33:9).

Reflection and Application

Over those years God brought healing to Esau's heart, allowing him to forgive. As a result he comes to Jacob with love, not bitterness. This could not have occurred when Jacob stole the blessing. The lack of forgiveness always leads to bitterness. I once knew an elderly woman in a church I attended who was very difficult to be around. She always wore black and had a scowl on her face. She exuded bitterness. She had few friends. A few years after I first met her I learned her story. Her fiancé had stood her up on their wedding day. She was never able to forgive him. This lack of forgiveness fed her bitterness that now extended to everyone around her forty plus years later.

Are there people I have difficulty forgiving for something they have done (or should have done) to me? Ask God to help you forgive them. Pray St Paul's prayer in Philippians 1:9-11 for that person. It is difficult to truly pray that prayer and still remain angry with them.

THE BLESSINGS OF ISAAC (GEN 27:1 - 28:5)

As Isaac ages his eyesight deteriorates to the point that he becomes blind. Like Abraham with Hagar, Isaac with Esau is spiritually blind to the will of God. Fearing that he is approaching death, he desires to give his children their blessings. He actually had at least thirty more years before he died. The two blessings are different. One is for the firstborn son, to be given to Esau. The other is the Abrahamic covenantal blessing, to be given to Jacob.

The blessing of the firstborn is one of prosperity and mastery over others. It calls for rain instead of famine, an often realized threat in Canaan as we see occurring in the lives of all three patriarchs. It specifies agricultural abundance which leads to prosperity. It desires nations to give allegiance. It ends with either a curse or a blessing on those who curse or bless Isaac's son (Gen 27:28-29). The blessing which Jacob steals is a material blessing. From the text it appears Isaac did not intend to give Esau the Abrahamic blessing, for it is not mentioned. The blessing Jacob later receives is a spiritual blessing. He receives the Abrahamic blessing as he is about to leave for Padan-aram (Gen 28:1-5). It is uncertain whether Isaac intended to give Jacob his blessing at the same time as Esau's or if in the turmoil after the theft was discovered it was forgotten. Given Isaac's relationship with Esau, he may not have even thought of Jacob. The text is silent on this. After Jacob's theft of Esau's blessing, Esau is given a blessing much different than the intended one. He will not find himself in fertile, well watered lands. He will be a man of war and will serve his brother. Yet at some point he will achieve freedom (Gen 27:39-40).

It is good to remember that Jacob's place in the covenantal line doesn't come from the stolen blessing in Genesis 27. It comes from the Abrahamic blessing in Genesis 28. As far as Jacob is concerned, that is the only important blessing.

One danger we all face is becoming so set in our ways, or determined that something turn out a particular way, that we can be blind to what God desires to do in our lives and in the lives of those around us. It's good to ask God from time to time, "Are my actions standing in the way of what you are doing?" Then take time to reflect on the question as he speaks to you.

JACOB'S THEFT OF THE BIRTHRIGHT AND
BLESSING (GEN 25:27-34; 27:5-27)

The accounts of the stolen birthright and blessing are two of the more sordid stories in the Bible. In it we see a duplicitous and lying son, a cunning manipulative mother, and a spiritually blind father. At this point we would not want to emulate any of them. The two scenes are separated by the sojourn in Gerar.

In the former Jacob steals Esau's birthright. Esau had gone out hunting possibly during the time of famine mentioned in Gen 26:1. After a day of unsuccessful hunting in the dry, thirsty land he was famished. The sight and smell of Jacob's stew induced him to trade his birthright for a bowl of the stew. The mention of Jacob cooking a stew is interesting. Hebrew, which is based on three-consonant roots, often can have different meanings for words having the same three letters. In this case *yazed* "to cook a stew" can also mean "to treat arrogantly," depending on the verb stem.[32] Putting these together, Jacob not only made a stew, but treated his brother with arrogance. Esau despised his birthright, thinking it of little value.

Jacob pretends to be Esau and when directly asked, lies and says that he is Esau. Rebekah shows herself to be related to Laban, her scheming greedy liar of a brother. Isaac—physically blind—also seems blind to the will of God. Based on all the dating given in the book of Genesis, the brothers were 77 years old at this time. They had had many years of living together. The result of Jacob's deception destroys any remaining relationship between the two brothers, with Esau threatening to kill Jacob.

The act of sin often involves hiding something. Jacob hides who he is from his father. Yet within the hour his deception is known. He didn't get away with his sin, and its effects were immediately felt.

Numbers 32:23 says, "Be sure your sin will find you out." Jacob's sin was found out quickly. How many times have ours been? Think of sins which you have committed that were discovered. How did it turn out? The knowledge that hidden sin is often discovered can be a deterrent that aids us when we are tempted to sin.

Jacob's theft of the blessing is ironic in a way. While he eventually becomes economically prosperous (Gen 30:43), he never achieves a position of power. He likely didn't consider his life to be blessed. He is taken advantage of by Laban (Gen 29:21-30; 31:4-7). At the end of fourteen years of working for Laban he has nothing. He is close to losing everything in the severe famine (Gen 42:1-2; 43:1-2). Rachel, his beloved wife, dies in childbirth (Gen 35:16-19). For years he thinks his beloved son, Joseph, is dead. His watches his sons have moral problems (Gen 34; 35:22; 38:15-19). In addition, they all are culpable in lying about what had happened to Joseph (Gen 37:31-35). He spends the last years of his life in Egypt, far from the land God had promised to him (Gen 47:5-6; 50:5). Upon meeting Pharaoh Jacob says that his life has been unpleasant (Gen 47:9). Life with his stolen blessing was not always easy for Jacob.

Reflection and Application ——————————————————————————————————

In the story of the stolen blessing, we observe one of the greatest effects of sin—the loss of relationship. Esau comes to hate Jacob, desiring to kill him. Jacob has to flee, most likely never seeing his mother again, and his father only near the end of his life (Gen 35:27-29). Likewise, in our lives sin, when it affects another, destroys relationships. We often hear in our society that it's OK as long as it doesn't affect someone else. But the reality is that sin, even when it is personal, always has communal effects. Someone else is always affected. Are there sins in my life that have ruined relationships?

As we look at this passage in greater detail another feature emerges: there is a changed relationship between Isaac and Rebekah. While their marriage began with love they seem to have grown apart. The Hebrew text of Gen 27:5 says that Rebekah accidentally overheard Isaac's directive to Esau. She wasn't listening in. This implies that Isaac hasn't talked with her about the intended blessing. Her subsequent actions bear this out. They also point out that she doesn't have a discussion with him about the giving of blessings. Rebekah is placed in a difficult situation, knowing from God's prophecy 78 years earlier that Jacob is the son to receive the Abrahamic blessing. We have seen Rebekah as a woman of faith, seeking out God during her difficult pregnancy. We have observed God's answer to her indicating that Jacob would be the chosen one. But now we see her lack of faith. As we saw with Sarah and Hagar, Rebekah takes matters into her own hands, not trusting God's timing. She arranges for Jacob to receive Esau's blessing. It ends with similar results, the loss of relationships.

Reflection and Application ———————————————————————

The loss of relationship experienced by Isaac and Rebekah is tragic. It caused estrangement between the brothers. Although the Bible doesn't say, Rebekah's conniving to make sure Jacob received the blessing must have had a negative effect on her relationship with Isaac. It points to the need to make communication with one's spouse a top priority for all of life.

REBEKAH-FINAL THOUGHTS

Looking at the story through Rebekah's eyes, several thoughts emerge. Given that she had problems with infertility and the fact that her sons are 77 years old means that she is well over 100. For 77 years she has been waiting in faith for the prophecy to be fulfilled. Has she somehow missed it? Is the delay in fulfillment her fault? The closeness she had with Isaac in the early years of their marriage, in the days when he was interceding with God for her, is gone. What happened? Likely Isaac's attempt to pass her off as his sister in Gerar has something to do with it. From the beginning of the story till the end there appears to be a gradual lessening of their relationship.

Now Isaac, in her eyes, is about to make a huge mistake. As she had when asked years ago if she would marry Isaac, she makes a quick decision, trying to fulfill the will of God for her younger son. Unfortunately, the cost of her decision leads to moral sin and a separation between her children. Were her actions right or wrong? The text doesn't give any judgment of her actions. It merely recounts the facts.

Rebekah struggled with the question we all struggle with. Should I wait for the Lord? Or is he asking me to do something? She took action. At times either is appropriate. Sometimes God desires us to wait on him. Other times he wants us to take action. When we do, it is important that our actions don't lead us into sin.

THE ROLE OF ELECTION–EXCURSUS

Much ink has been spent in discussing God's choosing Jacob and rejecting Esau. Malachi 1:2b–3a is often quoted in this regard. "Yet I have loved Jacob; but I have hated Esau." A closer look at the text suggests something different. The Hebrew word translated "hate" has a double meaning. While it can mean hate, it also can mean "love less." This is the sense that Jesus uses when he says that unless we hate our family we can't be his disciple (Lu 14:26). We must love him more than we love our families.

When Jacob and Esau meet years later, Jacob attempts to give Esau significant gifts of his herd of animals to appease him. Esau at first refuses, stating that he has plenty (Gen 33:9), feeling blessed himself. As Israel approaches the Promised Land at the end of the exodus, God tells them to not provoke the Edomites (Esau's descendants), for he has given them that land (Deut 2:4-6). God is protecting them. Later Moses tells the children of Israel not to detest the Edomites because they are their brothers (Deut 23:7). Just as God provided for Ishmael, although Isaac was the chosen one, so God provides for Esau, even though Jacob is the chosen one.

Reflection and Application ━━━

How would I characterize my love for God compared for my spouse or family? It is easy to say that we love God more, after all, what else are we supposed to say? But do I really? Is Jesus truly the center of my life?

THE SENDING OF JACOB (GEN 28:1-5)

As Jacob is about to leave for Padam-Aram Isaac gives him a blessing. This is in addition to the one Jacob stole from Esau. It is the covenantal Abrahamic blessing that had been given to Isaac—that he would be fruitful, becoming a company of peoples, and possessing the land promised to Abraham. In this way the blessing of Abraham that had been passed on to Isaac is now passed on to Jacob. He finally receives the blessing Rebekah had connived for him to receive after all, without having needed her help.

The decision to send Jacob away is based on the reality of the situation. There is the real possibility that Esau will kill him (Gen 27:41-42). Esau has too much respect for his father to carry it out while Isaac is still alive. Rebekah is afraid that they will kill each other (Gen 27:45). When Rebekah learns of Esau's threat, she devises a plan to send Jacob away. Unlike Isaac who had married within the ethnic clan, Esau had married two Hittite women (Gen 26:34-35). For some reason, whether religious or cultural, they didn't get along with their mother-in-law, Rebekah. It appears that Isaac was aware of this, for he listens to her plea to send Jacob back to Haran to find a wife. Interestingly, when Esau discovers that his parents aren't happy with his choice of wives, he marries one of Ishmael's daughters to try to get back into their good graces (Gen 28:6-9).

CHAPTER 3

Jacob, Rachel, and Leah

THE PROBLEM OF JACOB

Jacob is one of the more enigmatic people in the Old Testament. Some don't know what to think of him, wondering how God can choose a person such as him to be the head of what will become the nation of Israel. After all, he is a thief, a manipulator, a schemer, a swindler, a failure as a father and a flawed husband, truly a person of less than admirable character. Others don't like Jacob because his character hits too close to home. They see themselves in him. Yet God, in his wisdom, chose him. It is helpful to remember that the Bible doesn't always prescribe the way things should be, it describes what actually happened. It serves as a way to alert us by positive and negative examples of how we are to live our lives. It also points out how God works in people's lives and hearts to change them into the persons he desires them to be. This is the case with Jacob. Before Jacob can be renamed Israel, God has to bring healing to his life.

It is interesting to note that the prophet Micah associates Jacob with truth (Mic 7:20). God brings truth to Jacob. It is that Jacob doesn't belong to himself or family but to the Lord, the same Lord who bound himself to Jacob in a covenantal relationship.

JACOB'S DREAM (GEN 28:10-22)

Jacob begins the long 500 mile journey to Haran. Whether his dream experience occurs during his first night out is uncertain. It can't have been too long after leaving since he is still in Canaan. Bedding down for the night, with a rock for a pillow, he dreams. His dream consists of a ladder with angels ascending and descending, and God standing at the head of the ladder. God speaks to him, identifying himself as the God of Abraham and Isaac. He tells Jacob that he is giving the land to Jacob and his descendants. They will spread out throughout the land and all the families of the earth will be blessed through them. God reiterates the covenantal promise given to Abraham and Isaac. He confirms the covenantal blessing of Isaac and given to Jacob only a short time before. He promises to be with Jacob as he leaves the land of Canaan and guarantees his safe return.

While we would expect the angels to be descending to earth to be with Jacob and then ascending back to heaven this is not the case. They are ascending and then descending back to earth. It is as though one set of angels is identified with Canaan and another set with the land outside of Canaan. This fits with the ancient concept of territorial gods,—only in this case there is one supreme God, the God who stands at the top of the ladder and directs the angels.[33] When Jacob returns to the land of Canaan angels meet him. He says regarding the place they meet "This is God's camp". Interestingly he names the place "Mahanaim" meaning "two camps" (Gen 32:2). It's almost as if there are two camps of angels who meet him there as well.

There are two interesting things associated with this story. Throughout Jacob's life up to this point he has attempted to be in control of situations. In this account he is passive, being asleep. It is God who is in control. He, not Jacob, is in charge of the events taking place. He tells Jacob what will happen in the future. It is interesting that God causes Adam to be asleep when he creates Eve, Abraham to be asleep when he makes the covenant with him, and now Jacob when he affirms the covenant with him. It is God who makes it known to Jacob who is ultimately in control of both heaven and earth.

Jesus' statement in John 1:51 is also interesting. When Jesus has a dialogue with Nathanael he tells him "You will see the angels of ascending and descending upon the son of man." Notice they are first ascending and then descending, just as with Jacob. Jesus seems to be reflecting on Jacob's dream. He becomes the ladder which bridges heaven and earth. It's as though the angels associated with the Old Covenant are ascending back to heaven and those associated with the New Covenant are coming down to earth. It could also refer to Jesus ascending to heaven and descending at his second coming.

There are three aspects of God's speech to Jacob that are important: his presence, his protection, and the promise of a return. The presence of God is important throughout the Scriptures. God is present with his people. What encouragement that gives! He even tells Jacob "I am with you"—it is God himself, not one of the angels. God also promised to protect Jacob in his travels to Padan-Aram. In a world where it was thought that gods were territorial this would have seemed revolutionary. Jacob is not moving out of the territory controlled by YHWH into a territory controlled by another god, YHWH is going with him wherever he goes. In addition, God promises to bring Jacob back to the land of Canaan. It is God who later tells him to return (Gen 31:3).

Notice Jacob's response to the dream. He realizes that it is from God (Gen 28:16-17). This seems to be the first time he has an encounter with God, one which he will remember for the rest of his life. He creates a stele with the stone pillow and anoints it with oil, recognizing this spot as a holy place. He names it "Bethel" meaning "House of God" (Gen 28:19). He vows that if God will guide him on his journey and return him to his father, then this God who has spoken to him will be his (God Gen 28:20-22). He concludes by saying that he will give a tenth of whatever God prospers him with to God. Since there was no temple nor were their priests at this time, his tithe would have been in the form of a burnt offering. At this point he makes a spiritual decision. If the Lord does for Jacob all that he has promised, then the Lord will be his God.

Reflection and Application ————————————————————

How does the knowledge that God is with me impact my life? Does it make me less afraid of negative events which happen? Spend some time reflecting on God's presence and protection with you.

Although Jacob has knowledge of God, for he refers to him as Yahweh in Gen 28:16, he doesn't appear to yet have much of a personal relationship with him. His statement in verses 21-22 points out that it's not enough to know about God, we must have a personal relationship with him. As God continues to speak to him and influence his life in the coming years, Jacob will come to have that relationship. How would I characterize my relationship with God? Do I have a personal relationship with him? Or is my relationship more like Jacob's at this point in his life?

Jacob's tithe is an act of worship, giving allegiance to God in recognition of all the good things he has done for his worshipper. How do I look at my tithe to God? Do I see it as an act of worship or as more of an obligation?

JACOB IN PADAN-ARAM (GEN 29:1-14)

Jacob, in going to Padan-aram, was to seek the family of Bethuel the Aramean. The word "Aramean" is derived from the Hebrew word *ramah* which means "to deceive." Jacob has been a deceiver and swindler. He soon will meet up with Laban the Aramean who lives up to the meaning of his name. Like Abraham's servant before him, Jacob meets the person he is destined to meet at his arrival in Padan-aram. In both of these stories we see God at work. Statistically the chance that the first person either would meet is the intended one is small. That each would meet that person is almost impossible. God is certainly at work in their lives to make this happen.

Jacob also meets up with his uncle Laban, who is as manipulative and deceptive as Jacob, or more so, always trying to take advantage of Jacob. God arranges for Jacob to meet the one person who can show him by example what he himself is really like. It appears Jacob was truthful to Laban about his difficulties with Esau (Gen29:13).

Reflection and Application ————————————————————————————

God is at work in our lives as well. Many times we don't recognize it when it happens. Sometimes we realize it years later when looking back. It is worth keeping an eye out for ways God is impacting our lives.

JACOB AND HIS WIVES (GEN 29:15-35)

The love story of Jacob and Rachel is certainly no teen age heart throb story, Jacob being 77 years old when they meet. The text indicates his love for her was strong, so strong that serving her father for seven years before marrying her seemed a few days (Gen 29:20). But

Laban tricked him on the wedding day, giving him Leah as his bride instead (Gen 29:23–29). We can wonder how Laban's deception would have gone unnoticed. We can wonder why Rachel and Leah went along with it. Perhaps there is poetic justice here. Jacob, who had deceived his father, in his blind love for Rachel is deceived by her father. It is a moral commentary on Jacob's earlier deception. Since it was night and the bride was veiled Jacob likely didn't see his wife's face till the following morning. There is a rabbinic interpretive story enacting Jacob's and Leah's conversation the following morning that sets the scene well.

> "Said he [Jacob] to her [Leah]: 'You are a deceiver and the daughter of a deceiver!' 'Is there a teacher without pupils?' she retorted. 'Did not your father call you Esau, and you answered him! So did you too call me and I answered you.'"[34]

We can only guess at Laban's reasoning. Was it that because Leah's eyes were weak (Gen 29:17) that he thought her unmarriageable? Or was it merely a way to get another seven years of service from Jacob? Or was it really the cultural custom of marrying the eldest off first? We don't know. In any case Jacob ends up serving Laban for another seven years. The text says he loved Rachel more than Leah (Gen 29:30).

Jacob, the trickster, has been out schemed – out manipulated by Laban. He receives what he had dished out to Esau. In a way, his sin has found him out. In many ways the events surrounding his marriage to Rachel are Jacob's first steps on the path to righteousness. Rebekah had told Jacob to stay "a few days" with her brother (Gen 22:44). In an ironic twist, the same phrase describes Jacob's feelings about the time spent serving Laban which turned into seven years (Gen 29:20).

Reflection and Application ———————————————————————————————

As we have seen in the case of Abraham and now Jacob the Bible speaks of polygamy. It doesn't embrace the practice, merely reporting the fact that it occurs. This is true for many of the things reported in the Old Testament. The statement that Jacob loved Rachel more than Leah is an indictment of the ancient practice. Jesus makes a similar remark when he says "No man can serve two masters." It is a natural phenomenon to love one more than the other.

LEAH THE UNLOVED (GEN 29:30-35; 30:20; 31:14-16)

The only words Leah speaks are found in the naming of her sons, her answer to Rachel regarding the mandrakes, and her response when God tells Jacob to return to Canaan. Looking at those words can teach us much about her. In many ways she was trapped in a dysfunctional family, cultural standards, and community expectations. Throughout her life she faced many challenges and disappointments. She likely had poor eyesight (Gen 29:17). She had an arranged marriage, her father marrying her off by substituting her for her sister Rachel. We don't know what Leah's response to this deception was, but she apparently went along with it (Gen 29:23). She may have had no choice. Whether she had misgivings is uncertain. From Laban's cultural perspective the elder sister had to be married first (Gen 29:26). From the start of Leah's marriage things would not go well. Since having progeny was very important in the ancient world God saw to it that she, the unloved one, was blessed with children. The names she gives her children inform us about her emotional state concerning her relationship with Jacob. They also inform us of her faith. She names her first son Reuben, from the Hebrew root meaning "to see." In naming him she says "See, a son is born." She also says that the Lord has seen her. Note her plaintive hope. "Now that I have a son my husband will love me." It was not to be. She names her second son Simeon, from the Hebrew root meaning "to hear." This is the word from the Great Shema "Hear, O Israel …" She says her second son is due to God having heard her. When her third son is born she names him Levi, from the Hebrew root meaning "to attach." hoping that providing Jacob with three sons will make him love her more. She names her fourth son Judah, from the Hebrew root meaning "to praise."[35] By this point she has given up on being loved by Jacob. All she can do is praise God for all the children she has been given. The naming of Leah's last son points to her continuing frustration with her husband, saying with the naming "Now my husband will dwell with me because I have borne him six sons."

The naming of her sons shows the progression of her emotional state. It is obvious that she is aware that Jacob loves Rachel more than he loves her. Her hope that Jacob will love her at the birth of her firstborn suggests she was aware of the Abrahamic blessing of progeny. Giving Jacob a son would continue the family line. As the next two sons are born her hopes to be loved are diminished. The naming of Levi may indicate that for all of her married life to that point she feared Jacob would divorce her. Children would be a safeguard. She realizes with the birth of Judah that her hopes for love have been dashed. With the earlier births she speaks both of having the help of the Lord and of her hopes for Jacob to have a change of heart. Now she merely praises the Lord. This is the first occurrence in the Bible of a person praising God.

Her relationship with her family also suffers. Rachel becomes jealous of her because of her having children while Rachel does not. The relationship of both sisters with their father is tenuous. When Jacob talks with them about leaving they indicate they feel like foreigners, having effectively been sold by their father (Gen 31:14–15). In reality, he had abandoned them. She had to be disappointed in her sons. Four of them have moral problems: her eldest sleeps with her maid (Gen 35:22), her next two sons treacherously massacre the citizens of Shechem (Gen 34), and Judah, her fourth son takes a prostitute (Gen 38).

Coming from a family that didn't have an attachment to Yahweh, she developed a strong faith throughout her life. We can observe something about her faith in the naming of her sons. Their names imply she recognizes that God is with her, loves her, and provides for her and comforts her. God has seen and heard her, and she recognizes that it is God who has blessed her with children. When Jacob informs her that God has told him to return to Canaan, she tells him to do what God has told him (Gen 31:16). She has no reservations about leaving her home and family to go where God is leading.

Despite the fact that Jacob loved Rachel, at Leah's death she is buried in the family burial cave of Abraham (Gen 49:29–32). Leah and her handmaid become the mothers of ten of the twelve tribes of Israel. Jewish people today can trace their lineage to only two of the twelve tribes, Leah's sons Levi and Judah.

Reflection and Application ———————————————————————

Like Leah, we all face many challenges and disappointments. Our family dynamics may not be where we would like them to be. We face disappointments in our jobs and sometimes in our children. It is important to remember that God is with us. He comforts us and leads us as he did Leah.

RACHEL AND LEAH (GEN 30:1-24)

Given the great emphasis on having children in their society, a fierce rivalry develops between Rachel and Leah. But the story has a strange beginning given what God had told Jacob about having a large family. Both of his wives are barren. This condition affected all of the Patriarchal wives. It was God's way of telling Abraham, Isaac, and Jacob that he was the one who was blessing them. They could rely on him and his timing.

Eventually, due to Jacob loving Leah less, God opens her womb and she bears children (Gen 29:31-32). Rachel becomes extremely jealous of Leah for her fecundity (Gen 30:1). Her complaint to Jacob indicates the emotional state she was in: "Give me children or else I die." (Gen 30:1). Jacob, in anger, lashes out at her. Ironically her statement echoes Esau's statement to Jacob, "Give me food or else I will die." Rachel then makes the same response that Sarah had years earlier, telling Jacob to have children with her handmaid. Two children are born, Dan and Naphtali. The first is named Dan because, as Rachel says, "God has vindicated me." The naming of the second is more poignant. Rachel names him Naphtali because, she says, "I have wrestled with my sister and have prevailed." Jealousy reigns supreme! Rachel's and Leah's wrestling echoes Jacob's and Esau's wrestling in the womb and foreshadows Jacob's wrestling with the angel. Not to be outdone, Leah, now jealous of Rachel, does the same, giving her handmaid to Jacob as well. Jacob has two sons by Leah's handmaid, followed by Leah having two more sons and a daughter. Finally, after all these years, Rachel conceives and has a son, naming him Joseph taken from the Hebrew root *yasaph* "to add or increase." The significance of his naming is seen in her desire to have another son (Gen 30:24).

An ironic scene is found in Genesis 30:14-17 concerning the mandrakes. Mandrakes are roots from the potato family that have narcotic and purgative properties and were used in fertility rites (cf. Song of Solomon 7:12-13).[36] Rachel sells a night with Jacob to Leah in exchange for the mandrakes, thinking they might assist her in becoming fertile. It is reminiscent of the exchange between Jacob and Esau over the birthright (Gen 25:30-34). Leah's response is one of bitterness. "Is it a small matter for you to take my husband? And would you take my son's mandrakes also?" (Gen 30:15). The mandrakes don't help Rachel, but Leah conceives again. The story may also speak to how Jacob had been treating Leah.

It is interesting that Jacob doesn't suggest leaving Laban until Joseph is born (Gen 30:25). In that culture a barren woman could easily be discarded. Once Joseph is born, Rachel's status in Jacob's household is secure. Laban would have no worry about her future.

We don't know to what extent Jacob shares the covenantal blessing with his wives. If he does, it would help explain the rivalry that develops between them. Each wants to be the mother of the nation that would come forth. Each felt their worth was tied up in their children.

It is impossible to determine to what extent the rivalry between Rachel and Leah is a factor in the developing rivalry that we see in the lives of their children, but it likely has some impact.

Reflection and Application ———————————————————————————————————

We have no way of knowing whether the relationship between Rachel and Leah growing up was harmonious or was similar to that of Jacob and Esau. It is easy to see that once both were married to the same man an intense rivalry developed. The biblical injunction of Gen 2:24 for a man to cleave to his wife is based on the reality of what will happen when it's not followed. It would be interesting to know the percentage of divorces that occur due to the violation of this instruction.

The mandrake account shows how often we can attempt to take control in order to obtain the result we want. Rachel attempts to do this by obtaining Leah's mandrakes, to no avail. God is the one who has the ultimate control. He is the one who eventually opens her womb. What things have I attempted to control that I discovered really weren't within my control?

JACOB AND LABAN (GEN 30:25-43)

In many ways Jacob meets himself as he interacts with Laban. Both men have many of the same character traits. Both are scheming and manipulative. Both are untruthful. Jacob can easily see himself when he looks at uncle Laban. Laban tricks Jacob into serving him an extra seven years by giving him the wrong woman as his wife. Once Joseph is born Jacob desires to leave. He realizes that he has not benefited from all the years he has worked for Laban (Gen 30:30). Laban seeks to get him to remain (Gen 30:25-35). Jacob eventually agrees and their herds are separated based on color. Likely Laban has both the larger herds and those thought to be of more value. Given his personality, that may be why he so readily agreed to the arrangement. Jacob's use of the rods would have had no effect, likely being mostly magical belief. Visual inspection of the coloration and health of the sheep would have had a significant effect. Jacob had an eye for sheep breeding.

GOD'S PROTECTION OF JACOB (GEN 31:1-16, 41-42)

Due to Jacob's success in breeding his flocks, Laban's attitude towards him cools. Jacob's getting wind of this likely causes him to think of leaving again (Gen 31:1-2). At this point God tells him to return to the land of Canaan (Gen 31:3). His experience of the lack of communication between his parents apparently weighs on him, for he consults with his wives about leaving. Jacob calls Rachel and Leah to him, out in the fields away from Laban. His discussion with them tells us how he has begun to change. Five times he relates how God has helped him. This is no longer the trickster Jacob speaking. It is a man who realizes the hand of God upon his life. When Laban tries to cheat him, God intervenes (Gen 31:7). When Laban attempts to see that Jacob had the lesser flock, God sees that Jacob's flocks increases more than Laban's. Despite Laban's changing Jacob's wages ten times (Gen 31:41-42) God continues to provide for him. Through the years Laban has continually tried to take advantage of Jacob, trying to manipulate events. Jacob concludes that unless God had been with him throughout those twenty years, he would have left with nothing instead of the large herds he has.

Laban admits that he has it within his power to harm Jacob. This was a real possibility. God has to warn him in a dream not to harm Jacob. God continually is with Jacob. We see more of Laban's character in Rachel's and Leah's response. Both consider that there is nothing remaining for them in their father's house. The bride price paid by the prospective husband is reserved for their sustenance if their husband dies or divorces them. Jacob has worked for free instead. Laban hasn't made provisions to put what he has gained from Jacob's work aside for them. They consider him to have effectively sold them and taken the bride price, which should have been theirs, for himself. Their view that what God has taken away from Laban and given to Jacob belongs to them and their children. Based on their dealings with their father they have no reason not to leave.

The Hebrew verb *parats*, translated "prosperous" (Gen 30:43), speaks of a breaking away from limitations that have been placed on Jacob. It carries the meaning of spreading afar.[37]

It also occurs in Jacob's dream when God tells him that his descendants will spread in all directions (Gen 28:14). It then also occurs in Exodus 1:12, describing the expansion of the Israelites in Egypt. The Hebrew words translated "exceedingly" in Genesis 30:43 is the same word repeated twice, with the sense of "very very much"). The same words occur twice in God's covenant affirmation with Abraham (Gen 17:2, 6) and also in the Exodus account (Ex 1:7). The passages in Genesis speak to God's promise and fulfillment, with a foreshadowing of future fulfillment at the time of the Exodus.

THE FLIGHT FROM LABAN (GEN 31:17-42)

Jacob apparently has some fear of Laban, for he leaves secretly while Laban is away. Unknown to him, Rachel steals her father's household gods before they leave (Gen 31:19). Crossing the Euphrates River they head for Canaan. Learning of their flight, Laban pursues them, catching up with them seven days later. He accuses Jacob of taking away his daughters and stealing his gods. Jacob is incensed that Laban would think this of him, believing himself righteous in his dealings with his father-in-law (Gen 31:36-42). But there is something in the Hebrew text that the translations don't bring out. The Hebrew word *ganab* (to steal) occurs several times throughout the passage. It is the same word that is used in the seventh commandment "You shall not steal" (Ex 20:15). In Gen 31:20, 26, and 27 it is translated "deceived," while in Gen 31:19, 30, 32, and 39 it is translated "stole" or "steal." While Jacob doesn't see it this way, his deception is considered a theft by both the author of Genesis and by Laban. The Hebrew of verse 20 says, "And Jacob stole the heart of Laban." In verse 26 Laban says "You have stolen my heart." These verses speak of emotions. Just as Jacob stole Esau's heart in stealing the blessing, so now he steals Laban's heart by leaving in secret.

Reflection and Application ───────────────────────

Laban is grieved at not being able to give a proper goodbye to his daughters (Gen 31:27-28), feeling that Jacob has stolen his heart. What does it mean to steal one's heart? The seventh commandment (You shall not steal) is a call to honesty and uprightness in our dealings with others. To steal a heart is a grave sin. Stealing one's heart may not involve physically taking something belonging to another. In Laban's case it was stealing the opportunity to say goodbye to his daughters and grandchildren. It can be stealing another's reputation or denying them something extremely important to them. Have I ever stolen someone's heart?

THE CHANGED JACOB (GEN 31:36-42)

Jacob's defense of his actions tells us much about how he has changed over the years. He vigorously defends his character, not only to Laban, but also to other relatives of Laban who are able to verify his words (Gen 31:37). He asks Laban what his sin is, with the implication that he has been a faithful servant of Laban for the twenty years. He has taken excellent care of Laban's flocks and has assumed upon himself the cost of any of Laban's sheep killed by wild beasts. Given how many times Laban has tricked him, he could have easily exchanged tit for tat. Unlike his former self, he now appears as a man of integrity, confronting Laban with a clear conscience. He concludes with an acknowledgment that if it hadn't been for God's help, he would have gone away empty-handed. This is a much different Jacob than the young man we first meet.

During his long stay in Haran Jacob has dealt with many struggles. He has lived with the insecurities of Rachel and Leah as they both sought for his favor. He has seen the effect his inability to equally love his two wives has had on his family. He overcomes, with God's help, the manipulations that Laban used to take advantage of him. He also struggles with himself and his tendencies as he becomes more righteous. He is no longer a person who will walk over others to get what he wants.

Reflection and Application ———————————————————————————————

While Jacob has begun to change, there is still much more in his life that God will work on. In Jacob's acknowledgment of God's help we see the beginning of humility. There is a definite change in his attitude. At Bethel (Gen 28:20-21) he says that if this God who has appeared to him will protect him, he will follow him. There is a sense of uncertainty then. Now he has realized time and time again how God has actually been with him, guiding him. We can see that his relationship with God has changed.

It is helpful to know that God didn't give up on Jacob, just as he doesn't give up on us. How often as I go through life do I give praise to God for the good things that happen in my life? Do I see how he is guiding me?

Gen 31:6, 38-42 points to Jacob having a change of character. In his life we can see how a person is changed once God takes a hold of his life. This is most evident with people who have had a personal encounter with God later in life, but it is true no matter when we come to faith. What evidence is there in your life of God having changed you?

THE PARTING OF WAYS (GEN 31:43-55)

Laban considers everything Jacob has, including Jacob's family, as belonging to him. Yet for the sake of his daughters who are leaving his protection, he is willing for Jacob to keep what he has acquired (Gen 31:43). He suggests they make a covenant with each other. One significant part of the story is their eating with each other. It was a covenant meal, showing their acceptance of the covenant. Jacob and Laban are drawn together in a non-hostile familial agreement. Both pledge to do nothing to harm the other. A sacrifice draws God into the relationship as witness to their agreement. The following morning, after a farewell, both go their separate ways.

Reflection and Application ————————————————————————

Sharing of a meal had great implications in biblical times. It often meant acceptance and agreement with each other. It was also a sign of hospitality, something that we should practice more in our lives.

JACOB'S FEAR OF ESAU (GEN 32:1-23)

After parting from Laban Jacob continued down through Transjordan towards Canaan. As he approaches Canaan he is met by angels as he had been when he left Canaan twenty years earlier. It is interesting that he names the place Mahanaim, which means "two camps." It suggests there were two sets of guardian angels that met him—one set for when he was outside of Canaan and another within Canaan. He finds himself in a difficult dilemma. He has parted from Laban and can't return. He still has to face Esau. He sends a message to

Esau announcing his return. On hearing that Esau is coming to meet him, accompanied by four hundred men, he becomes deathly afraid (Gen 32:7, 11). He can't help but remember the reason he fled to Padan-aram in the first place. Esau had threatened to kill him over the stolen blessing (Gen 27:41). Is that still Esau's desire? Jacob's sin has come back to haunt him. He is consumed with fear as he anticipates meeting Esau. In desperation he prays to God for deliverance from his brother (Gen 32:9-12).

He also divides his camp into two groups, hoping that if Esau attacks him, one camp will be spared. Finally he puts together several sizable presents for Esau, sending them on ahead. In today's dollars, this would amount to around $711,000, more or less. By sending them in five separate batches he would know how Esau was responding before they actually met. Surprise attacks would be less likely as Esau would have stopped to take in each group of livestock. Also, Jacob's herders who would have returned with Esau would be a buffer. By this extravagant gift Jacob hopes to soften Esau's heart.

The makeup of his gifts is significant. Note that the larger group of each type of animal is female. This would allow for a faster growth of the herds. By this act Jacob emphasizes the return of the material blessing for prosperity that he stole from Esau.

The English text of Genesis 32:20 has Jacob saying, "I will appease him with the present." The Hebrew word for "appease" is the verb *kapfer* meaning "to cover up, atone". Most of the usages of the word in the Old Testament refer to making atonement. His present to Esau is more than a gift. By making restitution for stealing Esau's blessing of prosperity he seeks to atone for his sin. The goal is to seek reconciliation with his brother. Some have parsed the word "atonement" as "at-one-ment," indicating the unifying of relationship. The atoning work of Jesus on the cross was to bring us back into union with God, to make us one with God. (Although the English text doesn't indicate it, the Hebrew word *panim* meaning "face" or "presence" appears seven times in Gen 32:17-22). A direct translation of verse 20b might read "I will wipe [the anger from] his face with the gift that goes ahead of my face; afterward, when I see his face perhaps he will lift up my face…"[38] Each use anticipates the face-to-face encounter awaiting Jacob and Esau. It also anticipates the soon to happen face to face encounter with God.

There are several words in the text that tell of Jacob's changed attitude. He refers to himself as Esau's servant and Esau as his "lord" (Gen 32:4, 18). In his prayer to God he states that he is God's servant (Gen 32:10). In his eyes the stolen birthright has lost its value. With his actions he lets Esau know that the status of firstborn truly belongs to Esau. His repentance of his sins results in action. He gives reparations to Esau.

Reflection and Application ——————————————————————————

Notice the relationship between Jacob's sin against Esau and his fear. Sin often causes us to be fearful. It may be the fear of having our sin found out. It may be the fear of retribution. It can become paralyzing as we are always looking over our shoulder, afraid of what the future holds. The Psalmist in Ps 32:3-4 graphically tells of the effect of sin. "When I kept silent about my sin, my body wasted away through my groaning all day long. For day and night Thy hand was heavy upon me; my vitality was drained away as with the fever-heat of summer." (NASB). And all the time God is waiting patiently for us to confess our sin and give us absolution. Then we can move forward again. The Psalmist continues in verse 5 "I acknowledged my sin to Thee and my iniquity I did not hide; I said 'I will confess my transgression to the LORD.' And Thou didst forgive the guilt of my sin." Is there any fear presently in my life that is caused by sin? If so confess it and receive God's forgiveness and freedom.

When possible we should attempt to atone for our sins against others by making restitution. Restitution shows that a change of heart has occurred. It demonstrates the sorrow for sin and the desire to make things right.

There is something else here of note. The text says that Jacob was greatly afraid and distressed (Gen 32:7). His fear may hearken back to Rebekah's fear that the two brothers might kill each other. Not only is Jacob afraid that he might be killed, but also that he might kill Esau if their confrontation ends in a fight. Whoever might prevail in their fight could easily kill the other.

Reflection and Application ——————————————————————————

Whenever we find ourselves in a position to retaliate it is wise to remember Jacob's story. Retaliation always leads to further problems, whether physical or verbal. While we can make a right response, it can be for the wrong reason. We can also make the wrong response for the right reason. Rabbi Jonathan Sacks says on this passage, "In a conflict between two rights or two wrongs, there may be a proper way to act—the lesser of two evils, or the greater of two goods—but this does not cancel out all emotional pain."[39] *How often do I find myself seeking to retaliate against another for some fault they have committed against me?*

JACOB'S PRAYER (GEN 32:9-12)

When Jacob learns of Esau's coming with a band of men he is greatly distressed. He is afraid of being killed, with his wives and children either killed or enslaved. After dividing his camp he spends time in prayer. Looking at it in detail we can see several components. First, he prays to the God of his fathers (Gen 32:9). In doing so he makes the claim that God is his God too. Next, he reminds God that he told him to leave Laban and return to Canaan. It is a plea to be protected since he obeyed. Third, he recounts his own unworthiness to receive anything good from God and expresses gratitude for what God has done for him (Gen 32:10). Fourth, he asks for deliverance from the hand of his brother (Gen 32:11). Finally, he holds God to his own promises, with the implication that unless God does deliver him and his family, the promise will not be kept (Gen 32:12). Even though Jacob has made several plans for how to get on Esau's good side, he ultimately knows that God is the only one he can rely on.

His prayer tells us much about how he has changed. In his prayer we see his trust in God. Like his father and grandfather before him, he views God to be a trustworthy God, who stands on his word. The words of his prayer point to his growing awareness that it is not about what he can do and how he can manipulate things, but about who God is and what he can do.

Reflection and Application ————————————————————————

Prayer is the proper response in times of trouble. Throughout his life Jacob has learned this as he has struggled with Esau and Laban, and with Rachel and Leah. How do I respond in times of need? While it is good to make plans, as Jacob did, we need to always be aware that God is the only one we can really count on.

JACOB'S WRESTLING MATCH (GEN 32:24-32)

Jacob sends everyone across the river, and he is left alone with his fears. Who he actually wrestled with is a mystery as is the reason for the wrestling. It seems that it was unexpected. It is important that God, not Jacob, is the initiator. It is the longest wrestling match in history. Neither prevails against the other. Towards dawn the man dislocates Jacob's thigh, seeking to end their wrestling match. Jacob refuses to release him without receiving a blessing. This is significant as it indicates Jacob has come to the end of his self sufficiency. He finally humbles himself.

The man asks Jacob's name. Receiving it, he announces that Jacob's name will be changed to "Israel." Jacob asks the man's name but he refuses to give it. The man then blesses Jacob and leaves. The change of Jacob's name is significant. In Bible times names carried great meaning. The name not only identified the person, but it spoke of his character and identity. The name Jacob, known as the "heel grabber," comes from the Hebrew word *yakob* meaning "crooked." It describes the early Jacob to a T. The derivation of the name Israel is less certain, as it could be based on two different Hebrew words. It could be from the root *sryt* meaning "to struggle or prevail". It is more likely from the Hebrew word *yashar,* compounded with the name for God, *el.* *Yashar* means "straight, upright, law-abiding, honorable." In biblical usage it identifies a God-fearing, righteous person. This is what Jacob is becoming. In order to become "Israel" Jacob has to be transformed into a new person. His name change reflects that he is a man born to overcome.[40] The sun has set on the old Jacob at Bethel (Gen 28:11) as he is about to leave the land of Canaan. The sun rises on him now as he is about to reenter the land of Canaan (Gen 32:32). During this long twenty-year exile from his homeland God has been working on him. At Peniel he becomes transformed into a new person.

Although it is said he wrestled with a man, the prophet Hosea says he wrestled with an angel or messenger of God (Hos 12:4). Jacob realizes that he has wrestled, not with a man, but with God. Therefore, he names the place where they wrestled "Peniel," which means "face of God."

The giving of a name in ancient times meant that the receiver of the name was in control. By requesting his name, Jacob desires to regain control of the situation. Even though his sending gifts to Esau is an act of contrition, to an extent it still is an attempt to maintain control. This is a common problem that we face as well, the desire to be in control. But at Peniel Jacob learns that he isn't in control. He really isn't that self-sufficient.

Through his exile from Canaan and now at Peniel Jacob is transformed into a new person. The Apostle Paul speaks to the importance of our transformation in Romans 12:1-2. He speaks of the process of metamorphous, changed from one thing into another. How is my life being transformed? While names today don't have the same impact as in ancient times, we go by the name Christian. Do my character and identity match with the meaning of the word "Christian"?

When we go through times that are described as the "dark night of the soul," it is important to grab hold of God and not let go. At times when our prayers seem to bounce back off the ceiling, keep praying, keep holding on to God as Jacob did.

Cardinal Sarah says of this wrestling match, "This scene became the image for the spiritual combat and the efficacy of prayer. At night, in silence and solitude, we struggle with God in prayer."[41] Knowing God and forming an intimate relationship with him on a day-to-day basis requires effort. It never happens by osmosis. It requires wrestling. How much am I willing to wrestle to have an intimate relationship with God?

The 11th century Jewish commentator Rashbam connected Jacob's encounter with God with Moses' encounter at the burning bush (Ex 3:5) and Joshua's encounter with the commander of the Lord's army (Jos 5:13-15). He concluded that when something is important in a covenantal sense, God intervenes to see that it happens.[42] He does so here with Jacob. He will not allow Jacob to run away and fail, —so he wrestles with him. This was likely the nature of Jacob's wrestling. How would he respond to Esau? Would he try to avoid him, hoping things would work out, or meet him face to face?

One of the more difficult things we can face is the face-to-face encounter with someone we have wronged. We can easily find ourselves wrestling with the decision of whether or not to do so. Avoiding such a meeting can seem the easy way out, but it never solves anything. The face-to-face meeting is the only way to restore broken relationships. Have I ever wrestled with this issue? How did it turn out?

THE CHANGE IN NAME (GEN 32:27; 35:9)

In the Bible when a person is given a new name, he receives a new identity. Once Abram's name is changed to Abraham, he is never referred to again by the name Abram throughout the rest of the Old and New Testaments (Gen 17:5). When Saul's name is changed to Paul, he is never again referred to by the name Saul. This is not the case with Jacob even though the angel tells him his name will no longer be Jacob. He continues to be referred to as Jacob throughout the book of Genesis. The prophets refer to him as both Israel and Jacob. Why the difference? Although he is a new person, he still struggles against his earlier Jacob character. As Israel his life is transformed. May we all become an Israel.

We all face the same as our lives are transformed by Christ. Yet we can easily say with St. Paul, "wretched man that I am!" as we wrestle with the conflict between two natures in our lives. (Rom 7:14-25). It seems that Jacob faced this tension as well. It points to the need of examining our conscience to make certain we are not slipping back into the old ways.

The change in name helps identify the person Jacob wrestled with. The man tells Jacob his name is being changed to Israel (Gen 32:28). Later God tells him his name will no longer be Jacob but Israel (Gen 35:10-11). This links the wrestler with God.

We can wonder why Jacob's name had to be changed. It is because one's character and identity are tied up with his name that Jacob had his name changed. He is no longer a thief, liar, and a coward. After God's dealing with him during twenty-two years of exile, he is ready for a name change. He is willing to return to Esau what was rightfully his.

JACOB AND ESAU (GEN 33)

Despite all that has happened in the past few hours, Jacob is still uncertain of Esau's intentions. Therefore he again divides his camp based on his relationship with his children. Rachel's and Leah's handmaidens and their children are in front, Leah and her children next, with Rachel with Joseph in the rear, Rachel being his favorite. This arrangement shows his regard for his family. He has less regard for the children of Bilhah and Zilpah than for those of Leah, and the most regard for Rachel's. We can't help but wonder if the preferential treatment given to Joseph in this situation is a factor in his brothers' later hatred for him. How must the children of the two maidservants have felt, knowing that their father disvalued them enough to place them where they would bear the brunt of any attack by Esau! Jacob and Esau suffer under the parental treatment each had received in his youth. Jacob's children are now experiencing the same. In both cases, dysfunctional families are the result.

Jacob leads the procession to meet Esau. His actions show that despite all that God has done for him and has promised him, he still has some issues of faith. Like his grandmother who desired to help God with Hagar, Jacob devises a plan to protect at least part of his family and property in case Esau is vengeful. He has agonized over the past twenty years, dreading having a confrontation with his brother. He doesn't know that Esau is really coming in peace.

But a characteristic of Jacob's new character quickly emerges. He comes to Esau in total humility, bowing seven times before him. This is an act of homage that a vassal would show to his master.[43] By this act Jacob shows his acceptance of Esau as his lord. The intended blessing of the firstborn for Esau has been achieved (Gen 27:29). Jacob has the chance to demonstrate the humility he learned a few hours before at Peniel.

Esau has also greatly changed over the years. When we last saw him he was ready to kill Jacob (Gen 27:41). Now he embraces and kisses him (Gen 33:4). It is obvious that God has been working on his heart as well. This is seen in his running to meet Jacob. When Esau asks about Jacob's family, Jacob replies by attributing them to God's grace. He again acknowledges Esau as his lord.

We see Jacob losing his self-sufficiency, depending on God (Gen 32:11-12). Yet his faith falters because of his fear of Esau. In a moment of self-sufficiency he attempts to control the situation. How often do we find ourselves like him, gravitating between strong and weak faith? At the times when we find our faith weakening it is helpful to remember God's history with us. Since he has been there for us in the past, is there any reason for him to stop doing so now?

There are times when we can think that we are so bad that we can't change. The change in Esau from an impulsive narcissist who contemplated murder to a gracious, considerate man gives us hope. The work of God on a person's heart can change even the most hardened sinner.

When Jacob presses him to accept all the presents he is giving, Esau declines. He believes that he has plenty (Gen 33:9). In this he demonstrates a lack of selfishness. He finally accepts them after Jacob presses them on him. Jacob says something that seems a little strange at first glance: "for I see your face as one sees the face of God" (Gen 33:10). Jacob has been accepted by God. Now he has been accepted by Esau as well.

For some time Jacob and Esau live in close proximity to each other. But eventually, as both became exceedingly prosperous, they separate as Abraham and Lot had done earlier, for the same reason (Gen 36:6-8).

There is something else going on here that the Hebrew text suggests concerning Jacob and Esau (Gen 33:9-10). Notice in the account describing their meeting the number of times God is mentioned. Jacob mentions God three times while Esau doesn't mention him at all. When Jacob presses his gifts upon Esau, Esau literally says "substance (wealth) is to me plenty," indicating he is wealthy. In Hebrew this is *yesh li rab.* Jacob says *yesh li kol.* Only the last word is different. *Kol* means "all, everything." Jacob, by his choice of the word *kol,* indicates he attributes everything he has to God's graciousness. God has sufficiently cared for him and provided for him (Gen 33:5, 11). He has all he needs. In their responses, the two men display very different attitudes. While Esau's words seem abrupt and short, Jacob's are more refined, more polite. He effectively says, "No, please, if now I've found favor, then …" The difference in speech mannerisms between the brothers may be hinted at in Isaacs statement "the voice is the voice of Jacob but the hands are the hands of Esau" (Gen 24:22).[44]

To what extent are we like either Jacob or Esau? Do we see God's graciousness to be sufficient for us? Or do we like Esau focus on wealth?

THE RETURN TO CANAAN (GEN 33:18-20; 35:1-22)

Jacob and his family settle in Canaan for a short while before moving on to Bethel at God's command. Before they leave, something very significant happens. Jacob instructs everyone who is part of his household to dispense with all of their foreign gods. In addition, he tells them to get rid of their old clothing and to purify themselves. Everything related to their worship of foreign gods is buried under the oak of Shechem before they leave (Gen 35:2-4). Everything old is gone, they are beginning anew. At Bethel Jacob builds an altar in commemoration of God having spoken to him there and his pledge that Yahweh would be his only God if he aided him on his journey (Gen 28:20-22). Jacob realizes that Yahweh, the God of Abraham and Isaac, has truly been faithful to him. His requiring that all foreign gods held and worshipped by his family and retainers be discarded is a sign of a true conversion and allegiance to Yahweh.

Reflection and Application ──

When coming to Christ we are given a new life. It is important to bury the past. The sacrament of baptism signifies this. We are buried to our old life and raised to a new life. As we have looked at the Patriarchal families we have seen the difficulty they had in leaving their old gods behind. It is something the Israelites would struggle with throughout all of Old Testament history. It is the same struggle we face. We may not create physical representations at they did then, but our gods are just as real as the gods Jacob had his household discard. We struggle with the god of prosperity, materialism, narcissism, technology, sex, status, etc. What god do I have the most difficulty abandoning?

JACOB'S PASSIVE-AGGRESSIVE TENDENCIES (GEN 34)

Several things can be learned about Jacob in the events of chapter 34 which tells of the rape of his daughter. This will be covered in more depth when we look at Jacob's sons. But there is something that can be learned about Jacob in the account. His silence is intriguing. When he learns what has happened to Dinah, he does nothing. When he and his sons meet with Shechem's family, he remains silent, letting his sons do all the talking. Jacob only speaks at the end of the story when he upbraids his sons for bringing trouble upon him due to their action (Gen 34:30). His sons' comment is almost an indictment against Jacob for his inaction (Gen 34:31). Their reference to "our sister" in light of Jacob's doing nothing for "his daughter" may speak volumes. From his vigorous wrestling match just a short while ago we know his inactivity is not due to his being a senile, elderly man. He will continue to successfully rule his family for many more years. We have seen his previous passive nature in his relationship with his mother in the tent of Isaac. We have seen him acquiesce to Rachel and Leah in their entreaties for him to bear children with their handmaidens. We have seen him become more forceful in wrestling with an angel. Now he retreats to a more passive-aggressive stance. Thus, it is two of his sons who avenge their sister.

Reflection and Application ————————————————————————————————————

Passive-aggressive tendencies always result in the destruction of relationships. We have seen this in Jacob's relationships with his family.

THE DEATH OF JACOB'S WIVES (GEN 35:16-20; 48:7; 49:29-32)

It appears that all four of Jacob's wives die prior to their descent into Egypt. None of the four is mentioned in the list of Jacob's family who go down to Egypt (Gen 46:6-7). Rachel's death is described during the return to Canaan when she dies in childbirth (Gen 35:16–20). Some Jewish commentators see Rachel's death, her naming of her son, and Jacob's renaming him as being connected to the theft of Laban's gods. When Laban accuses Jacob of stealing his household gods, Jacob declares an oath that the person who stole them shall die (Gen 31:32). At that point he didn't know that Rachel had stolen them. Both Jacob and Rachel seem to remember this event when Benjamin is born. Rachel, knowing her death is near, names him Ben-oni (Gen 35:18). The Hebrew root *a-w-n* is associated with iniquity, trouble. The name could mean "Son of my iniquity." Jacob renames him Ben-jamin, meaning "son of the right hand." Since the right hand is associated with oaths, this could be reflection on his oath to Laban.[45] While it is uncertain whether or not Rachel's death is connected to her theft, the story does point out the consequences of sin.

At the end of his life Jacob mentions her death and burial near Bethlehem (Gen 48:7). According to Jewish tradition she would have been about 36 years old when she died. Some commentators suggest that Jacob's mentioning of her death in the middle of a discussion with Joseph about inheritance indicates Jacob never got over Rachel's death, grieving for her for the rest of his life. What effect her death had on Leah's future relationship with Jacob is unknown. But a comparison of Jacob's mention of Rachel and Leah on his deathbed provides a clue. The key phase is "to my sorrow" in the mention of Rachel's death and burial (Gen 48:7). It is an emotional response to her death, whereas his mention of Leah's death and burial seems more flat, a mere fact. From this it appears Leah never found the love she desperately desired.

Bilhah and Zilpah are not mentioned in the list of Jacob's family who descend to Egypt (Gen 46). Jacob, on his deathbed in Egypt, speaks of having buried Leah in the family tomb in Machpelah (Gen 49:29–32). This would have been prior to his going to Egypt.

JACOB'S FAVORITISM OF JOSEPH AND BENJAMIN
(GEN 37:3-4; 42:1 – 43:15; 44:27-29)

As with Jacob and Esau, parental favoritism was a problem. Jacob favored Joseph over his ten older brothers since Rachel was his mother. After Rachel's death (Gen 35:16–10), his love for Joseph and Benjamin likely increased compared to that for his other sons. The favoritism shown them will cause great harm in the future. As we have seen earlier, Jacob's favored love for Joseph began at his birth, continuing through the confrontation with Esau, and is shown in the coat of many colors (Gen 37:3).

The English translations describe Jacob as giving Joseph a coat of many colors (Gen 37:3). The Hebrew text is less clear as to its nature. It was likely similar to a coat worn by royalty.

This interpretation is supported by the brothers questioning if Joseph is to reign over them (Gen 37:8). It further fuels his brothers' hatred. Due to their hatred of Joseph, they sell him into slavery and tell Jacob that Joseph has been killed by wild beasts (Gen 37:28–36). Jacob refuses to be comforted by his children as he learns of Joseph's likely death. His grief would continue for many years before he would learn that Joseph was still alive. Although God used the selling of Joseph to further his glory, it was due to Jacob's sin.

In the account of Jacob's decision to send his sons to Egypt to buy food we again see his favoritism for Rachel's children. He refuses to send Benjamin, fearing his safety (Gen 42:4). We don't know Joseph's exact reasoning in his demand for his brothers to return with Benjamin. Was it because he longed to see his true brother? As a test of both his brother's and his father's feelings, Joseph keeps Simeon in prison and requires that Benjamin be included in their next trip to Egypt (Gen 42:19–20). Jacob categorically states that Benjamin will not be allowed to go with them, for with his brother dead Benjamin is all he has left. He also considers Simeon as well as dead, being imprisoned in Egypt. No mention is made that there are still nine other sons at home. It's as though Benjamin is all that matters. At this point Jacob's discussion with his sons ends. But time goes on and the famine continues. They are forced to return to Egypt for more food. Only the severity of the famine convinces Jacob to send them back. He still doesn't want to send Benjamin until Judah states that their trip will not be successful unless Benjamin is with them. Jacob upbraids his sons for telling the Egyptian official (Joseph) that they had a younger brother (Gen 43:6). He only relents, sending Benjamin with them, when Judah states that their trip will be useless unless Benjamin comes along and solemnly swears to be responsible for Benjamin. When Joseph threatens to keep Benjamin as a slave (Gen 44:17), Judah entreats him for mercy on behalf of their father. He recounts how Jacob has told them that if harm comes to Benjamin, the rest of his life would be filled with sorrow. The implication in Genesis 44:31 is that Benjamin's loss would result in Jacob's death.

Reflection and Application ————————————————————————————

Favoritism is a form of sin: It is the sin of idolatry. The favored one becomes idolized, often considered to never do wrong. In his early life, Joseph comes off as a spoiled brat. Such sin often contributes to others sinning as well, as we see in the case of Joseph's brothers. Do I love all of my children equally?

Are there sins that I commit that contribute to others being tempted to sin? If so, confess this sin to your pastor or priest, and also to the person you have led into temptation.

In the midst of this dilemma we see an aspect of Jacob's faith shining forth. Jacob, believing he has lost two sons, and fearing the loss of another beloved son, turns to God. He calls on *El Shaddai* (God Almighty) to protect Benjamin and bring him back. By doing so, he makes a break with the grief he has held for twelve or more years.

THE BLESSING OF JOSEPH'S SONS (GEN 48:8-20)

When Joseph is told that Jacob is near death, taking his two sons Manasseh and Ephraim, he goes to see his father. This leads to Jacob's interesting blessing of the two boys. Joseph stages their positioning before their grandfather, placing Manasseh's hand (the elder son) in Jacob's right hand and Ephraim's right hand in Jacob's left hand. Jacob deliberately reverses the positioning, placing his right hand on Ephraim's head and his left on Manasseh's head. When Joseph protests and tries to correct his father, Jacob says "no", stating that the younger son will be the greater of the two. This is borne out in the history of Israel, as the tribe of Ephraim was more prominent that the tribe of Manasseh. Throughout the Patriarchal narrative we have seen the unexpected. It is not the firstborn whom God chooses.

In the midst of his blessing Jacob says that the nation of Israel will pronounce this blessing: "May God make you like Ephraim and Manasseh" (Gen 48:20). What does this mean? Among the patriarchal families these are the first two brothers who are not characterized by jealousy and rivalry. The disharmony between Ishmael and Isaac was carried on by Jacob and Esau and by Joseph and his brothers. Through the years in Egypt the peace and forgiveness that Joseph came to experience in his heart is carried on by his sons. Thus the blessing "May God make you like Ephraim and Manasseh."[46]

Reflection and Application —————————————————————————————————

God desires that we have peaceful hearts, and that our homes be known for peace. If our homes are not centers of peace, our family members are not likely to be peaceful either. St. Paul says that one goal of the Christian life is that "the peace of God, which surpasses all comprehension, shall guard your hearts and your minds in Christ Jesus" (Phil 4:7). How do others see me? Am I known as a person of peace? If not, this will call for serious repentance and prayer.

JACOB IN EGYPT (GEN 46:1 – 48:7, 20-21; 49:28-50:14)

The words of Jacob in Genesis 47:9 are very interesting in light of his stolen blessing. He describes his life as being unpleasant, the exact opposite of what he tried to gain in his deception of his father (Gen 27:18-29). He lived seventeen years in Egypt (Gen 47:28). As his life approaches its end he asks Joseph to make sure that he is buried in Canaan (Gen 47:29-31). Like Isaac, he is blind at the end of life. He prophetically tells Joseph that his descendants will one day return to Canaan. After giving his sons a blessing, he passes away. After his embalming, the family returns to Canaan for the burial. Jacob is buried with Leah in the burial cave Abraham had purchased for the burial of Sarah (Gen 23:17).

Reflection and Application —————————————————————————————————

Jacob's description of his life points out how sin, which can seem so attractive when it happens, can come back to haunt us. Jacob sought to secure himself a blessing by deception. Reflecting on his life, he doesn't see a lot of blessing. He had been deceived by Laban, his father-in-law (Gen 29:21-25); manipulated by Laban (Gen 31:41-42); his beloved wife, Rachel, died at a young age (Gen 35:16-19; and he thought for many years that his favorite son, Joseph, was dead (Gen 37:33-35). If the same had happened to us, we likely would not feel very blessed.

CHAPTER 4

Joseph (Gen 37; 39-48; 50:22-26)

Joseph, like his father, is one of the more interesting characters in the book of Genesis. Like his father, God has to work in his life to make him into the person God desires him to be. Throughout his life many changes take place–from a spoiled brat to a slave, a prisoner and a leader and ruler of men. But it took time, many years, for this to happen. In his early years Joseph and his mother were favored by Jacob (Gen 33:2, 7). As we shall see, this favoritism continued throughout Joseph's life. He, like Isaac, is often considered to be a type of Christ.

Throughout the book of Genesis the phrase "These are the records of the generations of …" occurs many times. It serves as a bridge between two stories. Isaac has just died (Gen 35:29). Chapter 36 contains the genealogy of Esau. Now in Genesis 37:2 we have the transition from Jacob to Joseph. The remainder of the book of Genesis is concerned with the story of Joseph. The same phraseology occurs at the beginning of the New Testament: "The book of the genealogy of Jesus Christ" (Mt 1:1). This verse serves as a bridge between the Old and New Testaments, linking them together.

JOSEPH THE SPOILED BRAT (GEN 37:1-11)

From the various ages listed in the Joseph story, Jacob was likely around 91 years old when Joseph was born. According to Genesis 30 Joseph was much younger than his brothers, with the possible exception of Issachar and Zebulun who were somewhat closer to his age. By the time of the events described at the beginning of chapter 37 at least all but the last two of Joseph's brothers would have been grown men. The multicolored coat or tunic given to Joseph signifies that he has been given authority and honor. This may have led to 17-year-old Joseph giving four of his brothers a bad report, becoming a tattletale (Gen 37:2). These would have been Dan, Naphtali, Gad, and Asher. The coat and his telling on his brothers only heightens the animosity that his brothers feel towards him.

The Hebrew word for Joseph's coat occurs only one other time in the Old Testament. It is the same garment worn by David's daughter Tamar (2 Sam 13:18-19). It is interesting to note that in both cases the garment is stripped or torn, and the end result is tragic. From the account about Tamar it seems that Joseph's coat would have been something reserved for royalty. It's no wonder Joseph may have felt somewhat special and also receives his brother's hatred.

Reflection and Application ————————————————————————

The text doesn't say whether or not his brothers actually were doing something wrong, so we can't say whether Joseph was justified or not in telling on them. Again, we see the negative effect which favoritism has on relationships.

JOSEPH'S DREAMS (GEN 37:5-11)

In the ancient world dreams were taken very seriously, as it was thought that they contained information from the divine world. They were considered to be omens regarding the future. If given to a prophet they were considered divine revelation. For Joseph to have had two dreams projecting his rise to power over his brothers would have been taken very seriously. Given their father's favoritism for Joseph it is no wonder that his brothers resent him when they hear him recount his dreams. They hate him all the more after the first dream (Gen

37:8); after the second they become jealous as well (Gen 37:11). Jacob finally says something after the dream about the sun, moon, and stars, asking if all the family will bow to him, but does not take any action to guide Joseph (Gen 37:10–11).

Reflection and Application ——————————————————————————————

Joseph, growing up in that household, has to know how his brothers feel about him (Gen 37:4). He has to know that relating his dreams to them will worsen their relationship. Yet he proclaims the dreams, almost as though he is deliberately trying to antagonize his brothers. Knowing that after relating the first dream they hate him all the more, he still goes on to tell them the second dream. He seems to want to get their goat. Are there times that I try to deliberately antagonize someone or stir things up?

JOSEPH SOLD INTO SLAVERY (GEN 37:18-36)

In the following scene we see the extent of his brothers' hatred for Joseph. Over time their hatred continues to build until it reaches a tipping point. We now see them actually plotting his death on account of his dreams (Gen 37:20). We can wonder why Jacob sends him to his brothers. He must have known of their hatred. It is interesting to note that not only do they throw him into the pit, but they first strip him of his multicolored coat to signify how much they detest him. Only two of the ten brothers appear to have any reservations at all. Reuben pleads for not killing him, only throwing him into the pit, which they then do. He intends on rescuing him (Gen 37:21-22). When an opportunity arises, Judah suggests selling him instead of killing him. Judah appears to have authority over his brothers in that they agree to his suggestion. As a result Joseph is sold to the Ishmaelite traders who take him to Egypt and sell him into slavery to Potiphar (Gen 37:36). It is interesting to note that the Ishmaelites are likely grandchildren of Abraham. Yet there is no kinship recognition between them and Joseph's brothers. The descendents of Ishmael and Isaac are estranged from each other within only a couple of generations. It is not that much different today where most people don't know their third cousins.

In this account we see the devastating effect the sin of resentment can have upon a person. It festers and festers to the point we may do or say something we would never dream of saying or doing in our right mind. This is the place where confession is so important. We are able to repent and let go. Are there things in my life that I need to let go of?

Throughout the Patriarchal narratives sibling rivalry remains an issue. It occurs between Isaac and Ishmael. It occurs between Jacob and Esau. Now it occurs between Joseph and his brothers, with a more devastating effect. Siblings can often be at each other's throats, trying to outdo each other. How are my relationships with my siblings? Do we get along well or not? In my relationship with them is there anything I need to repent of and seek forgiveness?

The question facing the brothers now becomes, "What do we tell our father?" They decide to kill a goat and put its blood on Joseph's coat. Arriving home, they show it to Jacob, saying, "Examine, please" whether this is Joseph's coat (Gen 37:32). Likely Judah, who becomes the spokesmen for the brothers says this to their father. The Hebrew word *na'*, translated "please," often indicates an emotional response. It emphasizes the verb associated with it. In this case, Jacob is requested to examine carefully. He recognizes the coat and in mourning refuses to be comforted (Gen 37:35). These two words are significant, as we will see below.

The brothers' sin against Joseph affects more than Joseph and themselves. It affects Jacob as well. It is easy to sometimes rationalize that a particular sin isn't too bad because it doesn't affect someone else. That unfortunately is never true. Sin always has consequences. It may affect others who don't seem to have anything to do with the situation. Have there been sins I have committed that had unintended consequences for someone else?

JOSEPH'S LEARNING OF HUMILITY (GEN 39:1-23)

Before Joseph can become the man God wants him to be he has to learn humility. He has to spend time as a slave and as a prisoner before God can use him as the savior of Egypt and his own family. From being a prima donna he descends to a household slave. If that is not enough, he ends up spending three years in prison after being falsely accused. But throughout his ordeal, God is with him.

It is interesting to compare the two passages which speak of God being with Joseph in Egypt during his time of enslavement and as a prisoner. As a slave of Potiphar Joseph is successful because the Lord is with him (Gen 39:2-3). The Lord is also with him when he is imprisoned (Gen 39:21-23). Both passages contain the same Hebrew sentence, "And the Lord was with Joseph." At that point the two verses diverge. In Potiphar's household Joseph becomes successful since the Lord caused what he did to prosper in his hand. Joseph's actions are implied. When he is in prison the text says something different. He receives favor because of the Lord's kindness to him. "In his hand" is missing. This is significant. As a slave Joseph is successful because of both his exemplary actions and God's ongoing gifts to him. Potiphar recognizes them and gives him authority. But as a prisoner is becomes clear that God's supernatural actions account for his success. He can do nothing on his own.

The two-year time frame that Joseph is in prison is spoken of in Hebrew as "years of days" (Gen 41:1), as though Joseph is counting off the time day by day—days of suffering and anguish, discouragement, hoping to be remembered, having on-going disappointments. During this time he had to learn to trust God for everything, and come to know that God was with him.[47] It is based on this trusting relationship with God that he can eventually say to his brothers, "God sent me before you to preserve life" (Gen 45:5).

Reflection and Application

We all need to learn humility. Pride is one of the deadly sins. There are times God allows us to suffer in order to learn to depend on him. Are there times when I am tempted with pride? How has God has helped me to learn humility?

Joseph's character and actions are such that Potiphar recognizes the fact that God is with him. Do others see in my character and actions that God is with me?

THE TESTING OF JOSEPH (GEN 39:1-20)

Despite his favored upbringing, Joseph has developed good traits. This soon becomes clear to his master, Potiphar, who makes him the overseer of his household. Having this position, Joseph comes to the notice of Potiphar's wife, who repeatedly attempts to seduce him (Gen 39:7, 12). Joseph is in a dilemma. He is bound to obey the dictates of his master and his wife. Yet Joseph steadfastly refuses her advances, stating that to comply would be evil and sin (Gen 39:9). What is most interesting is his equating having sex with her as being sin against God! When she tries to force him, he flees. As a result, she turns against him, accusing him of attempting to seduce her. Potiphar, believing her lie, has Joseph thrown into prison (Gen 39:20). Joseph has gone from being the number one son to lying in a prison cell.

There is more going on in this story than it seems. It is a testing, much like the testing of Abraham when he is told to sacrifice Isaac (Gen 22:2). The Hebrew text which begins Gen 22:1 and Gen 39:7 ("and it came about after these things") is exactly the same, linking the two stories together. What's more, the next words in both passages, although spelled differently, sound almost exactly the same. *"Nasah"* (tested) sounds very much like *"nisa"* (lifted up). Joseph says that Potiphar has "withheld" nothing else from him. The only other incidence of the word "withheld" in the earlier portion of Genesis occurs when the angel tells Abraham that he has not withheld Isaac (Gen 22:12). A final link is seen in the word play over the name Isaac. The Hebrew word translated "make sport of" or "mock" (Gen 39:17) is *tsacheq.* The Hebrew for Isaac is *yitschaq.* The word can be translated either "mock" or "laugh;" Isaac's name means "laughter" (Gen 21:3-6).

What is the implication of these parallels? The author of Genesis is pointing out that the God of Abraham is the God of Joseph. God tests both of them to determine their devotion to him. Both at the beginning and the end of the Patriarchal narrative we see individuals devoted to God. In times of testing all of the Patriarchs–Abraham, Isaac, Jacob, and also Joseph– exhibit complete trust in God.

Joseph sets a good example for us in resisting evil and fleeing from it. Even though he might have personally profited from being in her favor, he refuses. He follows the dictates of Ps 119:30 "I have chosen the faithful way; I have placed thine ordinances before me." What temptations am I facing that I should flee from? At such times how do I show my trust and devotion to God?

JOSEPH THE INTERPRETER (GEN 40:1 – 42:37)

While in prison, Joseph has come to the attention of the chief jailer and is placed in charge of the other prisoners (Gen 39:21-23). When the cupbearer and the baker are imprisoned, Joseph is placed in charge of them. The text notes how observant Joseph is when these two men have their dreams. He notices that something is wrong. The Hebrew verb "observe" should be understood as "observing with perception." Joseph beholds that something is wrong. Had he not observed this he would likely never have questioned them and been able to interpret their dreams.

There is a significant difference between the interaction of Joseph with the two officials and his interaction with Pharaoh. Note that Joseph vaguely mentions God in his discussion with the two officials, yet he directly mentions that God is the interpreter three times in his discussion with Pharaoh. Why the difference? The cupbearer and the baker never ask Joseph if he can interpret their dreams. Joseph requests them to tell him, and they comply. Pharaoh specifically says he has heard Joseph can interpret dreams (Gen 41:15). Joseph has to correct him, stating that it is God who interprets dreams (Gen 41:16). When Joseph has heard Pharaoh's dreams he interprets them and gives him advice on what to do (Gen 41:33-37).

What makes Joseph successful? It is obvious that he has great talent, seen in his ability to govern the kingdom of Egypt during the seven years of famine. He had to have faced the temptation to take the credit for his success. In humility, he gives credit to God. Three times he tells Pharaoh that God is the one to whom credit is due (Gen 41:16, 25, 28). Pharaoh acknowledges this as he elevates Joseph (Gen 41:39). When Joseph identifies himself to his brothers, he clearly states that God has brought him to the position he has in Egypt (Gen 45:1-8). He never takes credit for himself.

We live our lives in the midst of a strange paradox. The times when we have the most reason to thank God are the times we can find ourselves least likely to do so. It is often tempting to take credit for our abilities and talents, especially when others attribute them to us. Doing so can easily turn into pride. We should always remember that all of our abilities, talents, and gifts come from God. It is he who has given them to us. We should give God the praise. What are times when I have had opportunities to give God the praise and haven't? Are there times I have taken all the credit myself?

JOSEPH AS PHARAOH'S REGENT (GEN 41:38-49)

As a result of Joseph giving God the praise for his ability to interpret the dream, Pharaoh decides to give Joseph the position. Pharaoh's words are very significant. He attributes Joseph's ability to God. Considering Joseph to be wise, he makes him second in command. Joseph's humility should be considered as a factor in Pharaoh's decision. He then renames Joseph and gives him the daughter of one of the Egyptian priests as a wife.

Like Abraham, Sarah, and Jacob, Joseph is given a new name. It is uncertain whether the name is Egyptian or Hebrew. Egyptologists are divided on its meaning. Jewish scholars, assuming that the name is Hebrew, have a meaning for this hyphenated name. "Zaphenath" is from the Hebrew root *tsaphan* meaning "to hide, treasure, or store up." "Paneah," from the Hebrew *pa'eah* means "to figure out or interpret". Thus Joseph's Egyptian name may mean "He who explains hidden things." It could also be translated (from a more Hebrew perspective), as "the revelation of the hidden."[48] This explains that the source of revelation is God, not Joseph, as Pharaoh views it.

THE NAMING OF JOSEPH'S SONS (GEN 41:50-52)

Like many Hebrew names, both Ephraim and Manasseh have great significance. They describe something related to Joseph's life. Joseph names his first son Manasseh, stating "for God has made me forget." His name is the participial form of the Hebrew verb *nashah*, meaning "forget." The name "Ephraim" comes from the Hebrew verb *parah*, meaning "to be fruitful." Joseph adds that his children are born in Egypt, calling it the land of his affliction. Given that he is now the second in command of all Egypt, why does he refer to it as a land of affliction? First, it is a place where he has been separated from his family. Second, it refers to the name Egypt itself. The Hebrew word for Egypt is a participial form of the verbal root *ts-r-r,* which has the meaning of limitation, binding, restriction. For later Israel, Egypt certainly became such a place.

Joseph's statement that God has made him forget his family is significant. He believes that his family has abandoned him. He knows the story of Ishmael and Esau, how God placed them off to the side in order to focus on the chosen son. Does the fact that his father never comes to Egypt looking for him mean he is like Ishmael and Esau? Joseph doesn't know that his father believes that he is dead. As he names his son "To Cause to Forget" he makes a break with his family and with the affliction which he has endured. He names his second son "Fruitful," indicating that he has overcome the years of affliction which he suffered.

FIRST MEETING WITH HIS BROTHERS (GEN 42:1-28)

The story of Joseph's meeting his brothers contains a bit of irony. His dreams of his brothers bowing down to him were a cause of their selling him into slavery. As they come before him, they bow down to him (Gen 42:6, 9). He notes this. But instead of identifying himself to them and embracing them, he remains aloof, accusing them of being spies. When they speak of having a younger son back home Joseph demands that the son be brought to Egypt as proof of their claim to be from a family. Joseph first states that all but one will be held in prison until the younger son returns. After holding them in prison for three days, he lessens the demand, only keeping Simeon in prison (Gen 42:24).

Behind the story of Joseph's meeting with his brothers there is a deeper story which has to do with their hearts. When Joseph angrily accuses them of spying, they talk among themselves, saying that because they got rid of Joseph, blood is required as payment (Gen 42:22). It is impersonal and passive. There is no mention of God being involved. As the story transpires, we see the brothers become more confused and fearful. When they discover the money, their hearts sink in trembling (Gen 42:28, 35). But at the same time there is the beginning of a spiritual awakening. They now begin to question what God is doing (Gen

42:28). One can wonder if this is the point where they begin to see that God is the one who has arranged everything. Although the text doesn't say so, we can wonder if Judah, whose life has been transformed, is the one to make the connection.

Reflection and Application ———

We can wonder why Joseph was so hard on his brothers at their first meeting. He seeks to learn how they have changed through the years. The answer won't come until their second journey to Egypt. God also uses this as a test; a test of Joseph's forgiveness and a test of the brothers' change of character. Are there things in my life that God is testing me in?

The discussion among Joseph's brothers shows us something significant. Although it is now several years removed from their selling Joseph they are consumed with guilt. They have no idea that they have been talking to Joseph, but their thoughts turn to what they did to him. Reuben has an "I told you so" moment. Joseph, overhearing them, weeps (Gen 42:24). This speaks to the forgiveness he has in his heart. Instead of having an "It serves you right" attitude, his heart goes out to them. At their leaving Joseph has the money they paid for the grain put back into their sacks. Upon finding it they are filled with dread. Their words suggest they tie all that has happened to them in Egypt to their treatment of Joseph.

Reflection and Application ———

Notice the effect of guilt upon Joseph's brothers. It has continued to haunt them day after day, year after year. If not for guilt they would not have made the connection to Joseph. Unconfessed sin continues to fester and can cause us to always be looking over our shoulder. It can haunt us for years. Is there unconfessed sin in my life that keeps cropping up in my mind? Confess it and receive absolution.

DELIBERATIONS CONCERNING RETURNING TO EGYPT (GEN 42:36 – 43:10)

As their supplies of food are diminished the family comes to the conclusion that they must return once again to Egypt for food. Jacob is still refusing to send Benjamin. Reuben rashly makes a vow, saying that if he doesn't bring Benjamin back Jacob can put his two sons to death. Effectively he is saying, "If you lose another son, then lose a couple grandchildren too." It goes nowhere. Judah reminds Jacob of the requirement to send Benjamin if they are to be successful. He finally says "send him with me. I will be responsible for him. I will bear the blame if I don't bring him back." Judah's authoritative word changes Jacob's heart on the matter, and he agrees to allow Benjamin to go with them.

JOSEPH'S SECOND MEETING WITH HIS BROTHERS (GEN 43:11-45:15)

When his brothers return to Egypt, Benjamin with them, they take several gifts to give to Joseph along with double the money that had been returned to them (Gen 43:11-12, 15). Twice the text mentions the doubling of the money. How easy it would have been to have ignored taking any money or only the exact amount they had found (Gen 42:35). This action speaks volumes to the changed Jacob. He is no longer the schemer, trying to get all he can for himself as he had when he stole the birthright.

The first thing the brothers attempt to do upon their arrival is to return the money. Joseph's steward tells them their God must have given it to them as he had received their money. This must have caused them to question what exactly was going on. Upon meeting Joseph, they give him the gifts they brought, bowing to him twice. Joseph arranges an interesting banquet with them. He seats them in their birth order, with Reuben at one end and Benjamin at the other. Although the Egyptians, including Joseph, sit by cultural custom at a separate table, the brothers are served from his table, with Benjamin receiving a portion of food five times that of each of his brothers (Gen 43:32-34). His brothers are dumbfounded at this. How could anyone there have known their birth order? (Gen 43:33-34). Why such special treatment for Benjamin? You can almost hear them whispering to themselves.

After the banquet, their sacks filled with grain, the brothers prepare to return to Canaan, believing that their quest has been successful. Simeon has been returned to them. Benjamin is with them. They soon will be reunited with their father. Unbeknownst to them, their money is returned to their sacks again, and Joseph's silver cup is inserted into Benjamin's sack. They leave at dawn but are stopped a short distance away and accused of theft. They protest, noting that they had even brought the money back from the first trip. Believing themselves innocent, they proclaim that if one of them had stolen the cup he should die and the rest become slaves. It is interesting to note that Jacob says much the same to Laban when he is accused of stealing Laban's gods. (Gen 31:32). In that case the guilty one (Rachel) goes free, while now the innocent one (Benjamin) is charged as guilty.

Joseph's steward says only the one who has stolen the cup will be enslaved, the rest will be free to return home. Beginning with the oldest their sacks are opened. Each of the brothers who were culpable in the selling of Joseph is shown to be innocent. Only the one brother who is innocent in relation to their sin is charged as being guilty. They return to the city and into Joseph's presence.

Judah becomes the spokesman for the group. His entreaty to Joseph will be dealt with in the chapter on Judah below. Joseph, unable to control himself any longer, with weeping identifies himself to his brothers (Gen 45:1–8). He then arranges for Jacob, with his possessions, to come to Egypt to live.

Why did Joseph go through all these machinations? It appears he was testing his brothers. Are these the same brothers who sold me into slavery years before? Would they take the same attitude towards Benjamin that they had towards me? Who would return? Would they leave Benjamin, with the other brothers returning to Canaan without him, abandoning Jacob's second favored son as they had me? Would only one or a few of the brothers return? They all return, pointing to a changed attitude on their part. As Judah pleads with Joseph to be allowed to take Benjamin's place, we see they have truly changed (Gen 44:30–34).

Reflection and Application —————————————————————————————

As we will see in Genesis chapter 45, Joseph has forgiven his brothers. But that doesn't mean that now they are suddenly best of friends. He still has doubts about them and their intentions that need to be examined. It is one thing to forgive, another to go on with life as though the sin had never happened. It takes time.

As Joseph identifies himself, he tells them not to be grieved at what they had done to him because he realizes that it was God who arranged all of it (Gen 45:5-8). Three times he tells them this. Weeping with joy he embraces each of them (Gen 45:14-15), which shows his forgiving and comforting nature. He doesn't bear a grudge. They don't need to be upset with themselves since God was the one who caused this to happen. Having forgiven them he can embrace them with joy. Joseph has a forgiving heart.

Reflection and Application ————————————————————————————————

Do I ever bear grudges? Is it possible to continue to bear a grudge and forgive someone at the same time? If anyone had the right to bear a grudge it was Jesus as he hung on the cross. His words are poignant: "Father, forgive them, for they do not know what they are doing." Jesus calls us to have the same forgiving heart. Do I have such a heart?

CHAPTER 5

⚮

Judah (Gen 38:1-30; 43:3-9; 44:14-34)

The story of Judah and Tamar is inserted right in the middle of the Joseph story. We can wonder why it is there and what it is really about. On the surface it doesn't seem to fit. But it is linked by the opening verse of chapter 38, "it came about at that time." The Hebrew text suggests a further reason for its inclusion. We will come to this, but first we must review the story itself. Judah had three sons, Er, Onan, and Shelah. Er had married Tamar; but died before she had children. According to the custom of the time, the passing on of one's inheritance to the next generation was important. Since Er didn't have a son, his line would end with him. One solution to this problem was levirate marriage, where the dead man's brother was to marry his brother's widow, with their first son being considered the heir of his deceased brother (cf. Deut 25:5-10). Onan, although taking his brother's widow, refuses to produce an heir for his brother, with the result that he also dies by the Lord's hand (Gen 38:10). From the text it appears that Shelah was still young when this happened. But when he becomes an adult, Judah refuses to allow him to marry Tamar (Gen 38:11-14). In the meantime Judah's wife has died.

Tamar is in a difficult situation. By sending her back to her father's house Judah has effectively removed her from his family. She is effectively engaged to Judah's son Shelah. By not making it official that Shelah will not marry her, she cannot remarry anyone else. She is in a no-win situation. Learning that Judah will be passing through the area where she is living, she pretends to be a prostitute. Judah has sex with her and she conceives (Gen 38:18). Tamar arranges for a kid goat to be sent to her as payment, receiving Judah's signet ring, cord, and staff as a pledge. Afterwards she dons her widow's clothing again and disappears. When Judah later finds out she is pregnant, he calls for her to be killed for prostitution (Gen 38:24-26). She asks him to examine the ring, cord, and staff which will identify the man who impregnated her. Judah recognizes them as belonging to him, declaring she more righteous than he is.

This is a very significant point in Judah's life. It begins his transformation. When Joseph's brothers bring his coat to Jacob it is most likely Judah who says "examine and see" (Gen 37:32). Tamar says exactly the same Hebrew words to Judah. The deceiver (Judah) has been deceived! These two verses contain the only occurrence of these two words together in the books of the law. Coupled with the fact that a goat is involved both in the deception of Jacob concerning Joseph (Gen 37:33) and in Tamar requesting a goat, it leads to Judah's acknowledging his sin. In saying that Tamar is more righteous than he is, Judah recognizes his sin. His statement indicates repentance. He recognizes his selfishness in protecting his son Shelah. He sees the tie-in with his earlier sin. His is the first confession of sin in the Bible.

His confession is freely given, not done under pressure, like when the prophet Nathan says to king David, "You are the man!" (2 Sam 12:7). In the society in which Judah lived his word would have been given more credibility than hers. After all she was a woman, a widow, and most likely a Canaanite. She had a much lower social status than he did. He could have denied responsibility and said it was her fault, much as Adam blamed Eve (Gen 3:12). Instead, he takes full responsibility, and repents. By doing so, his life begins to become transformed.

It is interesting that the name Judah is related to the Hebrew verbal root *lehodot*. This root has the meaning of "to thank or praise." It also has the meaning "to admit or confess".[49] Judah has admitted his sin. This is what makes him worthy to lead his brothers and become the progenitor of the Messiah (Mt 1:3).

How often does God trip us up, causing us to experience something which we have done in sin to someone else? It can be an effective way to confront us with our sin, leading us to repentance. Are there sins I have committed that God has brought to my attention by allowing me to experience the same sin?

Judah shows himself to have a repentant heart. How willing am I to confess when I sin and to repent?

There are other connections in this story which show the connection with the Joseph story. Judah and his brothers dip Joseph's cloak in the blood of a goat (Gen 37:31). Tamar wears a special garment and asks for a kid goat as payment. Rebekah kills two goats and has Jacob wear special clothes in the deception of Isaac (Gen 27:9, 15). God kills an animal to make garments for Adam and Eve after they sin (Gen 3:21). In each of these stories the killing of a goat and wearing special clothes are done to cover up sin. The story with Adam and Eve is somewhat different as God covers them as a result of their sin. In the other cases it is an attempt to keep sin from being known.

Judah has two sons who are killed by the Lord. Judah is responsible for Joseph being in Egypt. While in Egypt Joseph has two sons. Two sons are subtracted and two are added. It is interesting that in the debate about sending Benjamin, Reuben rashly says that if he doesn't bring Benjamin back, Jacob may kill his two sons (Gen 42:37). Why his sons and not himself? That two sons are mentioned is significant. There is a veiled reference here to Judah's not bringing Joseph home, as Reuben has attempted to do (Gen 37:22). Effectively he indicates that he is willing to experience the same punishment which Judah received (losing two sons) if he fails to bring Benjamin back.

With our fallen nature, our natural tendency is to try to cover up our sin. We don't want it to be known. How like Jacob and Joseph's brothers we are. Instead of confessing our sin we attempt to hide it, which often makes it worse when it comes out into the open. What sins have I tried to cover up? What was the result?

JUDAH'S INTERCESSION FOR BENJAMIN (GEN 44:16-34)

It is interesting to note that the text says Judah and his brothers returned to Joseph's house (Gen 44:14), pointing to the leadership role that Judah has acquired in their family. It is significant that in the genealogy of Christ the same phrase "Judah and his brothers" occurs (Mt 1:2). Judah's words speak to the same repentance and humility that he demonstrated in the Tamar episode. He says to Joseph, "What can we say? What can we speak? How can we justify ourselves?" He comes with a contrite heart. He recognizes God's involvement in what is transpiring. Although they are innocent of the sin of stealing the cup, God has found out their real iniquity. Judah identifies himself and his brothers with Benjamin, declaring that they also will be Joseph's slaves.

In the Jewish weekly readings Genesis 44:18 begins a new section. The previous section ends with the brothers admitting their guilt. The new section moves to Judah's passionate plea for Benjamin. Judah's speech leads to Joseph's revealing of himself to his brothers. After recounting the dialogue the brothers had with their father concerning Benjamin and the effect Benjamin's not being with them will have on their father, Judah willingly offers himself in Benjamin's place (Gen 44:33-34). Although innocent of the crime of which Benjamin has been accused, he willingly takes the penalty upon himself. In this sense Judah serves as a Christ-like figure.

Reflection and Application ————————————————————————————————

Judah's attitude is telling, since the brothers were not guilty of the crime they were accused of. Yet they knew they were guilty—only of a different crime committed many years earlier. We often find it easy to try to justify our actions before God. It is much better to come before God as Judah comes before Joseph; as we confront our own sin to say with Judah "What can we say? What can we speak? How can we justify ourselves?"

CHAPTER 6

The Blessing of Jacob
(Gen 48:8 – 49:27)

As Jacob is about to die, he gathers his family and gives them a blessing, based on his son's characters. Not all of them are blessings, as they contain prophetic elements as well. Some of the blessings dwell mostly on the past. Several are more future-oriented and hint at the tribes which descend from his sons. The author of Genesis notes that the blessings were given to the tribes descending from the sons (Gen 49:28).

But before he blesses his twelve sons, Jacob blesses Joseph's sons, Ephraim and Manasseh (Gen 48:15-16, 20). Due to Jacob's blindness, Joseph attempts to have Jacob's right hand on his eldest son, Manasseh, with his left hand on Ephraim. As the eldest, Manasseh would be the dominant one. But Jacob crosses his hands so that his right hand is on Ephraim, much to Joseph's consternation (Gen 48:13-14, 17-19). When Joseph tries to correct him, he refuses, stating that Ephraim, though the younger, would be the greater. He says he knew what he was doing. The blessing is prophetic. In the history of the nation of Israel, the tribe of Ephraim plays a much larger role that that of Manasseh. Jacob gives them a threefold blessing. He calls on the God whom Abraham and Isaac followed, the God who has been his shepherd throughout his long life, and the angel who redeemed him from evil to bless the two boys. The reference to the angel may look back to his wrestling with the angel before meeting Esau (Gen 32:24-32). The concluding verse of this section states that Jacob blessed each of his sons with an appropriate blessing.

REUBEN (GEN 29:32; 35:22; 49:3-4)

Reuben is Jacob's firstborn son and for all practical purposes he should have had special privilege in the family. But he is largely passed over. He appears to be impulsive; he makes rash oaths. He has good intentions but not the character to go with them. In his blessing Jacob describes Reuben as "uncontrolled as water" (Gen 49:3). His sin with Bilhah costs him his position in the family (Gen 35:22). When Jacob refuses to send Benjamin to Egypt, he rashly tells his father that Jacob can kill his two sons if he doesn't bring Benjamin back (Gen 42:37). His character is not that of the person God would have lead Israel. In the nation of Israel Reuben plays an insignificant role.

Status is not always based on birth order. Throughout Scripture we see this again and again, as often a younger son is chosen. Abel is accepted over Cain, Isaac over Ishmael, Jacob over Esau, Judah and Joseph over Reuben, David over his older brothers, etc. What is it that God sees in these men? It is their character. Three things are required for them to take a leadership role. First, they must have moral character, to stand up for what is right. Second, they must have a selfless attitude, willing to go to the aid of others. Third, they must have the ability to admit their mistakes, repent, and change direction. Of Jacob's sons Judah and Joseph definitely had these qualities, but the others not so much.

Reflection and Application ———————————————————————————————————

While there is always the opportunity for forgiveness from sin, sin always has consequences. It can affect us physically and emotionally. It is always costly. Remembering that sin has cost us can become a deterrent to sin for us. What costs have been associated with the sins I have committed?

SIMEON AND LEVI (GEN 34; 49:5-7)

The account of the rape of Dinah and the response of Simeon and Levi occurs in the middle of the journey to Bethel. It occurs during their stay at the city of Shechem where Dinah meets the prince Shechem who takes her by force. Whether his further attraction towards Dinah is truly love or is only of a political nature is uncertain. Several things in the text are of interest. Although we already know it, it says the Dinah was the daughter of Leah, not Rachel, Bilhah, or Zilpah. Leah is also Simeon's and Levi's mother, making Dinah their full sister in this convoluted family. It is the brothers, especially these two, who exhibit an emotional response. They are grieved and exceptionally angry (Gen 34:7). Several times in the story the relationship between the brothers and sister is brought up

Most of the characters in the story have moral culpability. Jacob is culpable for his silence at the rape of his daughter. Simeon's and Levi's righteous indignation is supplanted by their deception and excessive revenge, not only against Shechem, but also against all the males in the city, acquiring everything belonging to them, including their wives and children. The brothers also allow Shechem to marry Dinah and take her into his house before rescuing her three days later. Shechem is culpable for his actions in raping Dinah and his family for not condemning him for this act. Dinah and Leah appear almost as bystanders in the story.

Reflection and Application ————————————————————————

There are times when righteous indignation and anger are appropriate, as in the case of Dinah's brothers and Jesus' anger at the moneychangers (Jn 2:13-16). However, the brothers went beyond decency in their response. The danger occurs when our anger becomes obsessive and out of control. That can quickly lead us into sin. Is there anything I can become so emotionally angry about that I am in danger of sin?

JUDAH (GEN 49:8-12)

The blessings of Reuben, Simeon, and Levi were based on past events in their lives. Jacob now begins to turn to the future. He also begins to use animal-based metaphors in describing his sons. It is uncertain to what extent he is being prophetic. Although Joseph has the dream about his brothers bowing down to him (which they do Gen 42:6) Jacob indicates that his sons will bow down to Judah. This comes to fruition when David becomes king of all Israel. Judah is described as a lion, which the New Testament picks up on in calling Jesus the lion of the tribe of Judah (Rev 5:5). That Judah will rule is seen in the statement "the scepter shall not depart from Judah" (Gen 49:10). The identification of Shiloh is uncertain. With Judah being complicit in Joseph being sold into slavery and its cover-up, along with the incident with Tamar, Judah seems an unlikely fit to be the progenitor of the Messiah. But as we saw above, it was his repentance, his willingness to sacrifice himself for his step brother that made the difference.

ZEBULUN (GEN 49:13)

Zebulun is the final son born to Leah (Gen 30:20). This blessing is confusing since at no point did the tribe of Zebulun reach the coast of the Mediterranean Sea. Its territory was restricted to the western lower Galilee region. What is meant by Zebulun being a haven is uncertain.

ISSACHAR (GEN 49:14-15)

Issachar is the next to last son born to Leah (Gen 30:18). The tribe of Issachar lived in the fertile Jezreel valley, located between two mountain ranges. This makes sense of the mention of their existing between sheepfolds and in a pleasant land. Being on the north–south trade route meant that other nations would try to control the area, with the inhabitants often experiencing forced labor.

DAN (GEN 49:16-18)

Dan was the son of Rachel's maid, Bilhah (Gen 30:4-6). The tribe of Dan was allotted territory on the Mediterranean coast in an area controlled by the Philistines. Unable to subdue the Philistines, they eventually relocated to the far north (Jud 18). The name "Dan" and the mention of him judging is a play on words. Both are related to the Hebrew verb *dayan* "to judge." One item of note is the mention of Yahweh in verse 18. This is the only mention of Yahweh in the blessing. It is uncertain who is speaking here. Is it Jacob or Dan? The references to God in the Joseph blessing (Gen 49:24-25) are less direct.

GAD (GEN 49:19)

Gad is the son of Leah's maid Zilpah (Gen 30:10-11). The Hebrew of this blessing contains an extensive word play. Four of the six words of the text contain the Hebrew consonants G – D. The mention of "heel" in both the blessings of Dan and Gad may have some reference to Jacob's birth where he grabbed Esau's heel (Gen 25:26).

ASHER (GEN 49:20)

Asher was the second son born to Zilpah (Gen 30:13). The blessing given to him, like that of Gad, is so brief that it is hard to determine what is meant by the blessing.

NAPHTALI (GEN 49:21)

Naphtali iss the second son born to Bilhah (Gen 30:7-8). Like with Gad and Asher, the blessing is too brief to determine what is meant.

JOSEPH (GEN 49:22-26)

Whereas the number of words in the Hebrew text describing Gad, Asher, and Naphtali ranges from six to nine, the number of words describing Judah is 55 and the number describing Joseph, 61. The two sons who will come to have the greatest impact in the nation of Israel are given the most descriptive blessings.

The translations of the Joseph blessing are problematic. The NASB for verse 22 reads, "Joseph is a fruitful bough by a spring; its branches run over a wall." The RSV translates the verse like the NASB does. The NIV translates "bough" as "vines." They all use a plant metaphor. The Message translates it, "Joseph is a wild donkey, A wild donkey by a spring, spirited donkeys on a hill."[50] It uses an animal metaphor to translate the verse. The difficulty comes from the fact that the word translated "bough" is the Hebrew word for "son" and the word translated "branches" is the Hebrew word for "daughter." The derivation of the word translated "fruitful" could be either from the Hebrew word meaning "fruitful" or the word meaning "wild donkey." The context from the next line which speaks of archers suggests "wild donkey" is more likely.[51]

BENJAMIN (GEN 49:27)

Given Jacob's preference for Rachel's children, we might expect Benjamin to also have a longer blessing, but he also has only a nine-word blessing. The image utilized suggests that Benjamin would have warlike tendencies. This is seen in 1 Chronicles 8:40. It can also be observed in the descriptions of the war between Benjamin and the other Israelite tribes (Jud 20), in the civil war between David and the Benjaminites loyal to Ish-bosheth (2 Sam 2:12-32), and in the war of Rehoboam against Israel (I Kg 12:21). It was also noted that they were ambidextrous (1 Chron 12:2).

THE DEATH OF JACOB

As we noted above, Joseph has forgiven his brothers for selling him into slavery, saying that God sent him beforehand to save their lives (Gen 45:5-8). However, his brothers have great difficulty believing that Joseph has really forgiven them. Even after living in Egypt for seventeen years (Gen 47:28), they still have apprehensions. Fearing that Joseph still has a grudge against them they entreat him, in the name of Jacob, to forgive them (Gen 50:14-21). They had lived for seventeen years, unable to accept the fact that they were forgiven. How unfortunate! How sad! All these years they lived with unfounded fear.

Reflection and Application ————————————————————

It is easy for us to do the same, either with other persons or with God. Many people live with the sense that their sins are so great that God can't forgive them. They may confess the same sin over and over again, even though their sins have been forgiven and they have received absolution. Are there any sins I have confessed that I'm not sure I've been forgiven of? If so talk with your priest or pastor for guidance. God wants you to know that if you are truly repentant, you are forgiven.

EPILOGUE

As we have taken a look at the Patriarchs, one thing is clear. They were far from perfect. Each of the seven Patriarchs and Matriarchs failed at some point in their lives. Abraham, Isaac, and Jacob all had dysfunctional families. Each of them was deceptive at times. They could be manipulative. Each of their families contained bitter rivalries between siblings. Despite their many imperfections God chose to establish his covenant with them and through them to bless the world. There was no way they deserved his love, yet he gave it to them anyway. Their frailties, given to God, accounted for him doing amazing things through them. In the end they became the forefathers of the nation of Israel, God's chosen people.

Reflection and Application ───

This should give us comfort, as we are also imperfect people. We confront the same sins they did, and others beside. Yet our perfect God loves us just as he loved the Patriarchs. What hope this should give us as we walk in the same paths in which they walked.

ENDNOTES

1   Julia Blum, "Torah Portion in Real Time: Lech Lecha," *Israel Institute of Biblical Studies (blog),* October 18, 2018, https://blog.israelbiblicalstudies.com/jewish-studies/torah-portion-in-real-time-lech-lecha/

2   Julia Blum, "Biblical Portraits: Abraham (1)," *Israel Institute of Biblical Studies (blog),* June 13, 2019, https://blog.israelbiblicalstudies.com/jewish-studies/biblical-portraits-abraham-1/.

3   Cf. discussion of the "Religion of Abraham" in Walton, Matthews, and Chavalas, *The IVP Bible Background Commentary Old Testament* (Downers Grove: IVP Academic, 2000) pp 46-47.

4   Julia Blum,":Lech Lecha: The Journey Begins," *Israel Institute of Biblical Studies (blog),* November 5, 2020, https://blog.israelbiblicalstudies.com/jewish-studies/lech-lecha-the-journey-begins/.

5   Julia Blum, "Biblical Portrait: God Never Says "Oops", *Israel Institute of Biblical Studies (blog), July 3, 2019,* https://blog.israelbiblicalstudies.com/jewish-studies/biblical-portrait-god-never-says-oops/. Abram effectively says "I am *'ariri* by being `ariri*.

6   John H. Walton, *The NIV Application Commentary: Genesis* (Grand Rapids: Zondervan, 2001) p 420-422.

7   Ibid, p 428.

8   The Ugaritic literature points to the religion of the Canaanites being a fertility religion. Believing that sexual union of the gods and goddesses brought about fertility, ritual prostitution was practiced. What we know from the Ugaritic texts corroborate the Old Testament prophets condemnation of Canaanite practices.

9   Some Ancient Near Eastern marriage contracts of that time period actually stipulated that a barren wife should provide a surrogate child bearer. Cf John H. Walton, *The NIV Application Commentary: Genesis* (Grand Rapids: Zondervan, 2001), p 446.

10 John H. Walton, *The NIV Application Commentary: Genesis* (Grand Rapids: Zondervan, 2001), p 447-448.

11 Julia Blum, "Biblical Portraits: Sarah – A Painful Decision," *Israel Institute of Biblical Studies (blog), August 28, 2019,* https://blog.israelbiblicalstudies.com/jewish-studies/biblical-portraits-sarah-a-painful-decision/

12 Julia Blum, "Biblical Portraits: Sarah – Wandering And Wondering," *Israel Institute of Biblical Studies (blog), August 15, 2019,* https://blog.israelbiblicalstudies.com/jewish-studies/biblical-portraits-sarah-1/

13   John H. Walton, *The NIV Application Commentary: Genesis* (Grand Rapids: Zondervan, 2001), pp. 450-451 indicates that the rite of circumcision was commonly used in the Ancient Near East to mark a man's coming to puberty or marriage into the family of his bride. God uses this custom for a theological purpose—to show one's entry into the covenant community.

14   *El Shaddai,* usually translated "God Almighty," is related to the Hebrew word *shad* meaning "breast". The imagery draws on God as a comforter, giving care when needed.

15   When Paul speaks about their bodies being members of Christ, he asks if they should be taken away from Christ and made members of a harlot, concluding "May it never be!"

16   Nicholas J. Schaser, "What Got Sarah So Upset? *Israel Bible Weekly (blog), Israel Bible Center,* November 13, 2018, https://weekly.israelbiblecenter.com/got_sarah_upset/.

17   The sacrifice of Isaac, known as the *akeida*, is one of the most known texts in Judaism. It is read in Jewish New Year ceremonies (Rosh Hashana). The Jewish morning prayer includes; *Master of the Universe! Just as Abraham our father suppressed his compassion for his only son to do Your will with a whole heart, so may Your compassion suppress Your wrath against us, and may Your mercy prevail over Your attributes [of strict justice].*

18   Julia Blum, "What Did We Miss,? *Israel Institute of Biblical Studies (blog),* November 12, 2020, https://blog.israelbiblicalstudies.com/jewish-studies/what-did-we-miss-in-vayera/.

19   Bereshit Rabbah 56,4. Cf. also Mekilta de-Rabbi Ishmael, 90-95.

20   Julia Blum, "Unlocking the New Testament: The Lamb (2)," *Israel Institute of Biblical Studies (blog),* May 8, 2019.https://blog.israelbiblicalstudies.com/jewish-studies/unlocking-the-new-testament-the-lamb-2/.

21   J. D. Douglas, ed. The New Bible Dictionary (Grand Rapids: Wm B Eerdmans, 1965) p 107.

22   78 in the Old Testament, plus 6 more in the Apocrypha.

23   Julia Blum, "Unlocking the New Testament: The Lamb (2)," *Israel Institute of Biblical Studies (blog),* May 8, 2019, https://blog.israelbiblicalstudies.com/jewish-studies/unlocking-the-new-testament-the-lamb-2/.

24   The majority of the comparisons below are taken from Julia Blum, "What Did We Miss?" *Israel Institute of Biblical Studies (blog),* November 12, 2020, https://blog.israelbiblicalstudies.com/jewish-studies/what-did-we-miss-in-vayera/.

25   Matt Stromberg, "The Death and Resurrection of Isaac," *Property of Jesus (blog),* July 4, 2017, http://thepropertyofjesus.blogspot.com/2017/07/the-death-and-resurrection-of-isaac.html. He quotes two midrashic texts "Rabbi Judah says: When the sword touched Isaac's throat his soul flew clean out of him. And when… [God] let His voice be heard from between the cherubim, "Lay not thy hand upon the lad." The lad's soul was returned to his body. Then his father unbound him and Isaac rose, knowing that in this way the dead would come back to life in the future; whereupon he began to recite, "Blessed are You, LORD, who resurrects the dead." (Pirkei Rabbi Elieazer)
"By virtue of Isaac who offered himself as a sacrifice on top of the altar, the Holy One blessed be He, will resurrect the dead in the future…so that He may set them on their feet in the Age to Come". (Mekilta Simeon)"

26 Julia Blum, "Pardes, Two Sons of Abraham and Yom Kippur," *Israel Institute of Bible Studies (blog)* September 19, 2021, https://blog.israelbiblicalstudies.com/jewish-studies/pardes-two-sons-of-abraham-and-yom-kippur/

27 Yitzchok Schochet, "Is Faith a Reality? Explore the essence of faith," *Chabad.org (video),* Date unknown, https://www.chabad.org/multimedia/video_cdo/aid/3559212/jewish/Is-Faith-a-Reality.htm.

28 John H. Walton, *The NIV Application Commentary: Genesis (*Grand Rapids: Zondervan, 2001) p 530 notes that a thirsty camel can drink as much as 25 gallons of water. With a water jar holding about three gallons, to water all the camels could take 80 to 100 drawings of water.

29 Julia Blum, "Biblical Portraits: Rebecca (2)," *Israel Institute of Biblical Studies (blog),* July 20, 2017, https://blog.israelbiblicalstudies.com/jewish-studies/biblical-portraits-rebecca-2/.

30 Julia Blum, "Biblical Portraits: Rebecca (3)," *Israel Institute of Biblical Studies (blog),* July 27, 2017, https://blog.israelbiblicalstudies.com/jewish-studies/biblical-portraits-rebecca-3/.

31 Her brother, Laban, worshiped household gods (Gen 31:19).

32 Julia Blum, "New Testament Reflections: Toledot," *Israel Institute of Biblical Studies (blog),* November 28, 2019, https://blog.israelbiblicalstudies.com/jewish-studies/new-testament-reflections-toledot/.

33 Julia Blum, "Torah Portion in Real Time: Vayetze," *Israel Institute of Biblical Studies (blog),* November 15, 2018, https://blog.israelbiblicalstudies.com/jewish-studies/torah-portion-in-real-time-vayetze/ says that the Jewish commentator Rashi holds to the view of two sets of territorial angels. One set were for Palestine, the other for the land north of Palestine. Each provides protection for the territory they govern.

34 Eli Lizorkin-Eyzenberg, *The Hidden Story of Jacob* (Jerusalem: Israel Bible Center, 2019), 34.

35 It is interesting to note that the Hebrew verb *lehodot* from which Judah's name is taken also has the meaning "to admit or confess," which comes into play in the interaction between Judah and Joseph over Benjamin. Cf. Julia Blum's article on this. Julia Blum, "High Holy Days: Gates of Repentence," *Israel Institute of Biblical Studies (blog),* September 24, 2020, https://blog.israelbiblicalstudies.com/jewish-studies/high-holy-days-gates-of-repentance/.

36 Walton, 588.

37 Eli Lizorkin-Eyzenberg, *The Hidden Story of Jacob* (Jerusalem: Israel Bible Center, 2019), 39.

38 Lizorkin-Eyzenberg, 62.

39 Lizorkin-Eyzenberg, 50.

40 Lizorkin-Eyzenberg, 53-4.

41 Robert Cardinal Sarah, *The Day Is Now Far Spent* (San Francisco: Ignatius Press, 2019), 31.

42 Lizorkin-Eyzenberg, 55-56.

43 Lizorkin-Eyzenberg, 59.

44   *Israel Institure of Biblical Studies (blog),* Date and author unknown, https://lp.israelbiblicalstudies.com/lp_iibs_dhb_different_speech_eml-en.html?cid=77817&adGroupId=-1&utm_source=Email_Marketing&utm_medium=Jacob_Esau_Voices_02_20&utm_campaign=BIB_EN_EML_Jacob_Esau_Voices_2020-02-16_77817&commChannel=1&stid=3286048&hash=8c711e522d796b9e2a26a81bd11eb0ab&_at=0.3.9919853,0.135720834.z3fdxta3dda2pshuap&_atscid=3_2483_135720834_9919853_0_Tz3fdxta3dda2pshuap.

45   Julia Blum, "Things Of Heaven And Of Earth," *Israel Institute of Biblical Studies (blog),* December 2, 2020, https://blog.israelbiblicalstudies.com/jewish-studies/things-of-heaven-and-of-earth/

46   Julia Blum, "Christmas Torah Portion: Vayechi," *Israel Institute of Biblical Studies (blog),* December 20, 2018, https://blog.israelbiblicalstudies.com/jewish-studies/christmas-torah-portion-vayechi/ This is still continued in the Jewish blessing for sons. The blessing for daughters is "May God make you like Sarah, Rebecca, Rachel, and Leah".

47   Julia Blum, "Torah Portion in Real Time: Miketz," *Israel Institute of Biblical Studies (blog),* December 6, 2018, https://blog.israelbiblicalstudies.com/jewish-studies/torah-portion-in-real-time-miketz/

48   Julia Blum, Torah Portion in Real Time: Miketz," *Israel Institute of Biblical Studies (blog),* December 6, 2018, "https://blog.israelbiblicalstudies.com/jewish-studies/torah-portion-in-real-time-miketz/ (accessed 2/10/2020).

49   Julia Blum, "Torah Portion in Real Time: Vayeshev," *Israel Institute of Biblical Studies (blog),* November 29,2018, https://blog.israelbiblicalstudies.com/jewish-studies/torah-portion-in-real-time-vayeshev/.

50   Peterson, Eugene H, *The Message: The Bible in Contemporary Language* (Colorado Springs: NavPress, 2005), p. 87.

51   The difference depends on whether the Hebrew root is P-R-', or P-R-H.

ABOUT THE AUTHOR

David Hasey has spent his career leading Bible studies and teaching biblical related classes. He is the author of "Selah! Devotionals that will Cause You to Stop and Think" In this book he combines his training in Ancient Biblical Studies with his passion for Bible studies. He has an M-Div and MA in biblical studies from Trinity Evangelical Divinity School.

Printed in the United States
by Baker & Taylor Publisher Services